THE GIRL WITH THE DRAGON TATTOO

AND

PHILOSOPHY

The Blackwell Philosophy and Pop Culture Series
Series Editor: William Irwin

THE GIRL WITH THE DRAGON TATTOO

AND

PHILOSOPHY

EVERYTHING IS FIRE

Edited by Eric Bronson

WILEY

John Wiley & Sons, Inc.

Copyright © 2012 by John Wiley & Sons, Inc. All rights reserved

Published by John Wiley & Sons, Inc., Hoboken, New Jersey

Published simultaneously in Canada

Chapter opener design by Forty-five Degree Design LLC

For general information about our other products and services, please contact our Customer Care Department within the United States at (800) 762-2974, outside the United States at (317) 572-3993 or fax (317) 572-4002.

Wiley also publishes its books in a variety of electronic formats and by print-on-demand. Some content that appears in standard print versions of this book may not be available in other formats. For more information about Wiley products, visit us at www.wiley.com.

Library of Congress Cataloging-in-Publication Data:

  The girl with the dragon tattoo and philosophy: everything is fire/edited by Eric Bronson.
    p. cm.—(The Blackwell philosophy and pop culture series; 40)
  Includes bibliographical references and index.
  ISBN 978-0-470-94758-6 (pbk.: acid-free paper); ISBN 978-1-118-13291-3 (ebk);
  ISBN 978-1-118-13292-0 (ebk); ISBN 978-1-118-13293-7 (ebk)
    1. Larsson, Stieg, 1954–2004—Criticism and interpretation. 2. Philosophy in literature. 3. Larsson, Stieg, 1954–2004. Män som hatar kvinnor. 4. Larsson, Stieg, 1954–2004. Flickan som lekte med elden. 5. Larsson, Stieg, 1954–2004. Luftslottet som sprängdes. 6. Larsson, Stieg, 1954–2004—Philosophy. I. Bronson, Eric (date).
  PT9876.22.A6933Z67 2012
  839.73'8—dc23
                                                                2011034588

Printed in the United States of America

10 9 8 7 6 5 4 3 2 1

To Pippi Longstocking and the misfit in all of us

Everything great is done in the storm.
—Plato

CONTENTS

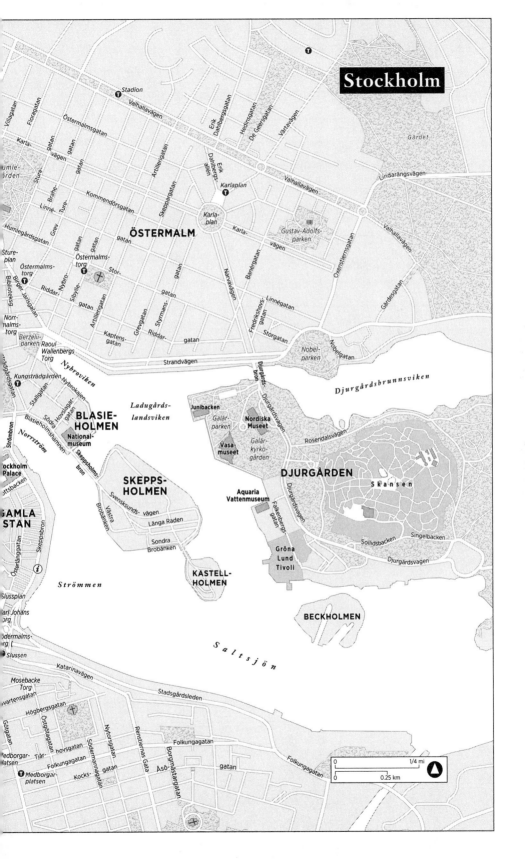

Stockholm

Gärdet

Stadion
Valhallavägen

Villagatan
Floragatan
Östermalmsgatan
Karla- gatan
vägen
Sture-
Brahe-
Linné- Ture-
Kommendörsgatan

Humlegårdsgatan
Grev-
Humle-
gården

Sture-
plan
Östermalms-
torg

ÖSTERMALM

Erik Dahlbergsgatan
Hedinsgatan
De Geersgatan
Värtavägen

Erik Dahlbergs allén
Artillerigatan
Skeppargatan

Karlaplan

Karla-
plan

Karla-
vägen

Valhallavägen

Lindarängsvägen

Gustav-Adolfs-
parken

Oxenstjernsgatan

Valhallavägen

Gärdesgatan

Riddar- gatan
Nybro-
Sibylle- gatan
Stor-
gatan
Artillerigatan

Östermalms-
torg

Narvavägen

Bandgatan

Gärdesgatan

Norr-
malms-
torg

Kaptens-
gatan
Greygatan
Styrmans-
gatan
Riddar- gatan
gatan
Strandvägen

Linnégatan

Fredrikshovs-
gatan
Storgatan

Nobel-
parken
Nobelgatan

Berzelii-
parken Raoul
Wallenbergs
Torg
Nybroviken

Djurgårds-
bron

Djurgårdsbrunnsviken

Kungsträdgården
Nybrokajen
Stallgatan

**BLASIE-
HOLMEN**

Ladugårds-
landsviken

Junibacken
Galär-
parken
Nordiska
Museet

Djurgårdsvägen

Södra Hovslagar-
Blasieholmshamnen

Strömbron
Norrström

National-
museum
Skeppsholms-
bron

Vasa-
museet

Galär-
kyrko-
gården

Rosendalsvägen

Stockholm
Palace

**SKEPPS-
HOLMEN**

Svensksunds- vägen
Västra Brobänken
Länga Raden

Sondra
Brobänken

Aquaria
Vattenmuseum

DJURGÅRDEN

Skansen

Djurgårdsvägen
Falkenbergs-
gatan

**GAMLA
STAN**

Skeppsbron

Strömmen

**KASTELL-
HOLMEN**

Sollidsbacken
Singelbacken
Djurgårdsvägen

Gröna
Lund
Tivoli

Slussplan
arl Johans
org

dermalms-
rg

Slussen

BECKHOLMEN

S a l t s j ö n

Mosebacke
Torg
vartensgatan

Katarinavägen

Stadsgårdsleden

Högbergsgatan

Östgötagatan
Nytorgsgatan
Renstiernas Gata

hovsgatan

Folkungagatan

Borgmästargatan

Folkungagatan

medborgar-
latsen
Tjär-
Folkungagatan
Kocks-
gatan
Åsö-
gatan

Medborgar-
platsen

0 ————— 1/4 mi
0 ————— 0.25 km

ACKNOWLEDGMENTS

Confidential Sources

Like all good detective stories, this book has a confusing and complicated cast of characters who intersect in magical ways and fill the words on the page with their living pulse. As Lisbeth Salander and Mikael Blomkvist quickly discover, no one person can go it very far alone.

The authors of this volume, my fellow Knights of the Philosophic Table, shared an "obsessive determination" to work long hours in the spirit of Kalle Blomkvist. They never lost their patience and joy in putting their cumulative wisdom to work on Lisbeth's behalf. To them, I'd like to pass on the thoughtful words that Blomkvist's sister Annika says to Lisbeth after they go through their trial together: "Go and get some sleep. And stay out of trouble for a while." And before your tail-lights disappear around the corner, let me also say, "Thanks."

Everyone should have a Blomkvist playing bass in his band. The guy who flawlessly kept the time when the rest of us went off on our riffs was Bill Irwin. Like Blomkvist, Bill is also a fiercely loyal friend, and professionally, he is "almost pathologically focused on the job at hand. He took hold of a story and worked his way forward to the point where it approached perfection. When he was at his best he was brilliant . . ."

Thanks also to Connie Santisteban over at Wiley. Although publishing houses often resemble the Section's top secret office in Östermalm, where "employees have no idea of the others' existence," Connie gives it all a personal touch. And like Erika Berger in charge at *Millennium* and later at the *Svenska Morgon-Posten*, Connie runs the show creatively, decisively, and compassionately.

Over at York University, where the Canadian Dags and Mias meet for coffee and contemplation, two people deserve special recognition. Thanks to Patrick Taylor, who, like Dragan Armansky, takes in the outcasts and firmly believes, "Everyone deserves a chance." And thanks also to Gail Vanstone, who, in following Dag's footsteps to *Millennium*, gave me the tip that blew the whole thing open.

Finally, thanks to Dave Tulloch and the new Bronson women: Elana and Sophie. Like Lisbeth's long-distance friendship with Plague, Poison, and SixOfOne at Hacker Republic, if I "could claim to have any sort of family or group affiliation, then it [is] with these lunatics."

INTRODUCTION

The Girl Who Kicked the Sophists' Nest

If Lisbeth Salander is the new voice of reason, then truth "can be a moody bitch."

I suppose Stieg Larsson approved of this droll characterization from his hard-boiled, coffee-swilling journalist, Mikael Blomkvist, but it's a bit of a problem for old-school philosophers.

Ever since Socrates, philosophers have been enamored with the belief that Truth (with a capital T) is unchanging, indivisible, and immortal. For more than two thousand years, we've taken comfort in that worldview. "Truth is beauty, beauty truth," said the poet John Keats in 1819, studiously pondering a Grecian urn.

Yet Lisbeth is not classically beautiful. Created in the image of another great Swedish sleuth, Pippi Longstocking, Larsson's heroine is "pale and anorexic," "a stray cat,"[1] with red hair dyed black that, even when cut short, "still stuck out in all directions."[2] Dragan Armansky, the levelheaded boss of Milton Security, eloquently describes his first impressions of Lisbeth: "She looked as though she had just emerged from a week-long orgy with a gang of hard rockers."[3]

Lisbeth's lack of interest in beauty is more than skin deep. Her friend and occasional lover Mimmi Wu tells us that "Salander had no taste whatsoever." Besides her "disgusting dirt-brown sofa,"[4] Lisbeth's "apartment in Stockholm might look like a bomb had gone off in it."[5] When she can afford a fancy new apartment decorated in any tasteful way she chooses, Salander spends 90,000 kronor . . . at IKEA! At least she pays to have the furniture assembled at home. (Who knew you could do that?)

And yet truth, if not beauty, is constantly on the mind of this antisocial girl with the dragon tattoo who exposes the misogynists, the chauvinists, and the bigots of high society. When Larsson first submitted *The Millennium Trilogy* to his Swedish publisher, all three books went under the title *Men Who Hate Women* (a title preserved in the Swedish edition). Larsson's trilogy is part courtroom thriller, part espionage intrigue, and part murder mystery, but at its root, Salander's story is the truth "about violence against women, and the men who enable it."[6]

Despite its universal appeal, Larsson's tale is a distinctly Swedish story, with Stockholm at the center. Salander and Blomkvist may battle neo-Nazis in the freezing snow of Hedeby or snuggle up to Elvis music in Blomkvist's rustic cabin in Sandhamn, but Larsson's characters always come back to Stockholm. That's why the Stockholm City Museum gives *Millennium* tours to Larsson fans, pointing out apartments and coffeehouses described in the books. It's also why the last image in the final Swedish film, *The Girl Who Kicked the Hornet's Nest*, is a panoramic view of Stockholm. In Columbia Pictures' Hollywood remake, Rooney Mara replaces the wonderful actress Noomi Rapace and Daniel Craig takes over for Swedish cinema icon Michael Nyqvist, but director David Fincher understood that for the story to work, it needed to be filmed in Stockholm.

Like Lisbeth in Stockholm, Socrates saw himself as a gadfly in Athens, an annoying pest who forced the city sophists to look deeper into their own hypocrisies. Before Lisbeth, it was Socrates who was brought to trial and preconvicted in the court of public opinion. "I have incurred a great deal of bitter hostility," he complained, "and this is what will bring about my destruction." Salander puts it differently. "Every time I turn around," she says in *The Girl Who Played with Fire*, "there's some fucking pile of shit with a beer belly in my way acting tough."[7]

In the book you hold in your hands, the Athens of Socrates and the Stockholm of Salander come together. We realize that you may not have studied philosophy and that you may not have a kooky Uncle Gustaf who spins wise, moralistic tales on Walpurgis Night. (Bummer for you.) So to that end, we've assembled a team of philosophers from the United States, Canada, England, France, and yes, Sweden, to help us sort the Fords from the Fjords. With them, we'll investigate why we can't seem to get enough of this antisocial, psychologically damaged hacker with a photographic memory. We'll consider whether journalists and hackers are the new philosophers and, if so, whether they will suffer the same hemlock backlash. We'll wonder why Lisbeth eats Big Macs at McDonald's and Billy's Pan Pizza at 7-Eleven when there's fine lamb to be had at Samir's, and the Bosnian burek is all the rage in Fridhemsplan. This, and much, much more.

Inspector Figuerola might have dabbled in philosophy and the history of ideas before taking down the dirty Nikolich brothers, but we're going to need to dig a little deeper here. You'll probably want to stock up on junk food and Marlboro Lights and grab some coffee. Lots of it. Because philosophers don't suffer fools kindly, and with Salander and Blomkvist in the mix, you can be sure that some of those a—holes are going to get hung out to dry.

You've seen the T-shirt: CONSIDER THIS A FAIR WARNING.

NOTES

1. Stieg Larsson, *The Girl with the Dragon Tattoo*, trans. Reg Keeland (New York: Vintage, 2009), pp. 38, 40.

2. Stieg Larsson, *The Girl Who Played with Fire*, trans. Reg Keeland (New York: Vintage, 2010), p. 103.

3. Larsson, *The Girl with the Dragon Tattoo*, p. 38.

4. Larsson, *The Girl Who Played with Fire*, p. 136

5. Larsson, *The Girl with the Dragon Tattoo*, p. 380.

6. Stieg Larsson, *The Girl Who Kicked the Hornet's Nest*, trans. Reg Keeland (New York: Alfred A. Knopf, 2010), p. 514.

7. Ibid., p. 511.

PART ONE

LISBETH "THE IDIOT" SALANDER

The cyborg is a creature in a post-gender world.
—Donna Haraway

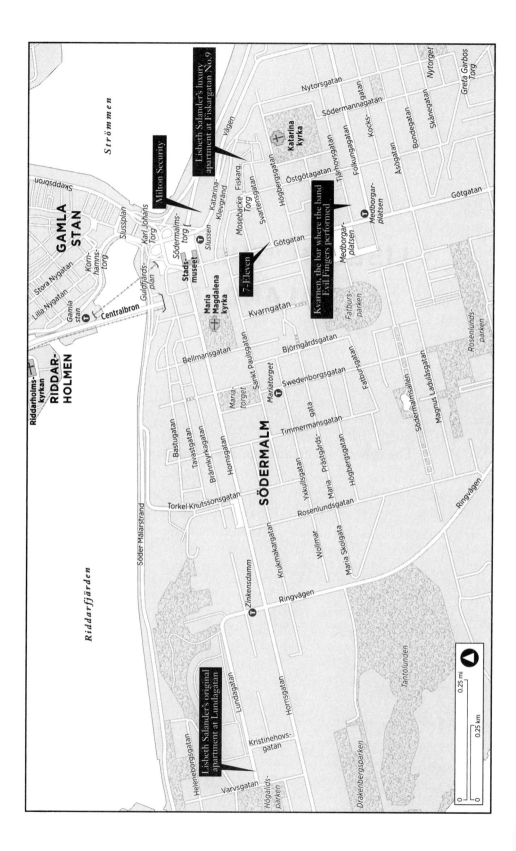

LABELING LISBETH: STI(E)GMA AND SPOILED IDENTITY

Aryn Martin and Mary Simms

Lisbeth Salander is *"a sick, murderous, insane fucking person. A loose cannon. A whore."*[1] At least, that is what Advokat Bjurman thinks after combing her official record. In just one brief conversation, Dr. Teleborian describes her as "psychotic," "obsessive," "paranoid," "schizophrenic," and "an egomaniacal psychopath."[2] In the wake of her institutionalization at St. Stefan's, she is characterized as mentally ill and, at the age of eighteen, declared legally incompetent. Even her allies, Holger Palmgren and Mikael Blomkvist, throw their hats into the diagnostic ring with speculation that Lisbeth has Asperger's syndrome. Lisbeth Salander is a magnet for labels.

The impetus for this labeling frenzy is Lisbeth's uniqueness in both biography and character. Her father is a Russian spy who is protected by an overly zealous secret section of the Swedish government. Her entanglement with the mental health system resulted from an elaborate and unprecedented conspiracy. She is a diminutive hacker genius accomplished at kickboxing but hopeless at small talk. We readers are invited to sympathize with Larsson's heroine because of her fantastically raw deal. In the exhilarating court scene in *The Girl Who Kicked the Hornet's Nest*, Salander's lawyer, Anita Giannini, tramples Dr. Teleborian as she demonstrates that Lisbeth is "just as sane and intelligent as anyone in this room."[3] This victory puts Lisbeth back on the right side of the asylum's doors, as her declaration of incompetence is rescinded, then and there. Sanity prevails.

Yet Larsson's heroine may not be so exceptional after all. In his classic books *Stigma* and *Asylums*, Erving Goffman (1922–1982) showed us that people are shaped by their social situations. Goffman argued that once institutionalized—whether in a prison or a psychiatric hospital—"inmates" share certain experiences and adaptations owing to their social location (and not because of their inherent illness or badness). After leaving these institutions, former inmates bear the discrediting mark of having been there: the label of "mentally ill," "incompetent," or "criminal." This stigma, Goffman argued, powerfully shapes their subsequent social encounters, whether their stigma is known or hidden.

By drawing attention to the vehemence with which people and institutions repeatedly label Lisbeth, Larsson covers much of the same ground as Goffman. He illustrates the ways in which labels come to stand in for and eclipse the person. He shows that there is slippage among discrediting labels, so that we are more likely to believe, for example, that someone labeled mentally ill is also prone to violence, promiscuity, or substance abuse. Once someone enters the bureaucratic machinery of a psychiatric institution, behaviors that would go unnoticed in "normals" are recorded as symptoms of illness. Finally, we see that labels solidified in official state records are called into play in subsequent incidents, strengthening one another like so many spools of barbed wire.

Perhaps the most powerful lesson we learn from Lisbeth's labels is about the incongruity between the paper version of a discredited person and her flesh-and-blood self. It seems that Lisbeth is victimized and later vindicated only because she was *wrongly* labeled. Yet if we read the *Millennium* series as being only about one person's raw deal, and we feel triumphant when she is restored to freedom, we miss something important. This reading ignores countless people—the so-called *rightly* labeled—whose stigma appears justified. And that's a problem. It's never okay to reduce people to the less-than-human status prompted by easy labels.

The Right to Remain Sullen

Although we don't know much about Lisbeth's time in St. Stefan's (aside from the fact that she hogged the sensory deprivation room), Goffman described a number of rituals common to such institutions.[4] "Abasements, degradations, humiliations, and profanations of self" radically change the victims' view of themselves and others.[5] First, inmates are cut off from the outside world and from the roles they occupied outside of the institution. No longer daughter, student, or sister, the psychiatric inmate is a patient only, subordinate to staff around the clock and in all physical spaces. The time spent away from roles "on the outside" can never be recovered. Admission procedures such as "photographing, weighing, fingerprinting, assigning numbers, searching, listing personal possessions for storage, undressing, bathing, disinfecting, haircutting, issuing institutional clothing, instructing as to rules, and assigning to quarters" turn the patient into a standardized object.[6] We can imagine that it would be particularly traumatic for a young Lisbeth to surrender what Goffman called an "identity kit," the cosmetics and the clothing that people ordinarily use to manage the guise in which they appear to others.[7]

Goffman discussed in detail many other "attacks on the self," including forced social contact necessary to group living and lack of control over decision making, scheduling, finances, nourishment, and movement. A key practice that characterizes life in a psychiatric institution is that everything is written down. We know this was true of Lisbeth's stay at St. Stefan's because the records are available for Giannini to count the days Salander spent in restraints. The casebook archives every aspect of an inmate's history and hospital life in a form readily available to all manner of staff members but often not to the patient herself. Although record keeping seems an obvious, sensible, and benign convention, Goffman highlighted some of its worrisome effects. Patients are not in a position—as are those of us on the "outside"—to manage personal information in social interactions. When talking to others, we routinely tailor which bits of ourselves to share, which to hide or downplay, and which to exaggerate. If we have an embarrassing lapse of judgment, we can choose not to tell anyone or to spin it in a favorable and rational light. Psychiatric patients, however, might find that this mistake is just the kind of detail that would be recorded as a symptom of illness and thrown back at them should they attempt to present themselves to staff or fellow patients as "normal."

Instead of constructing a "self-story," as we all do, the mental patient's story is already constructed by others and written along psychiatric lines. Lisbeth's casebook "was filled with terms such as *introverted, socially inhibited, lacking in empathy, ego-fixated, psychopathic and asocial behavior, difficulty in cooperating,* and *incapable of assimilating learning.*"[8] Each action and adaptation of the patient is scrutinized and recoded in psych-speak. "[T]he official sheet of paper," Goffman wrote, "attests that the patient is of unsound mind, a danger to himself and others—an attestation, incidentally, which seems to cut deeply into the patient's pride, and into the possibility of having any."[9]

What we know about Lisbeth's time in St. Stefan's maps eerily onto Goffman's account. At first, she tries to explain to doctors and other support workers her mother's abuse and the reasons for her retaliation against her father. She finds she isn't listened to. Goffman wrote of the mental patient: "The statements he makes may be discounted as mere symptoms. . . . Often he is considered to be of insufficient ritual status to be given even minor greetings, let alone listened to."[10] We can imagine that Lisbeth's lowly social status and hence her invisibility are exacerbated by the added social failings of being female, small, and practically a child.

Lisbeth's response to being ignored is silence:

> *Why won't you talk to doctors?*
>   Because they don't listen to what I say.
>   She was aware that all such comments were entered into her record, documenting that her silence was a completely rational decision.[11]

Teleborian later calls this silence "disturbed behavior."[12] Silence, withdrawal, and sullenness are all predictable responses of mental patients to their social situation, although Lisbeth's lifelong extension of this behavior to every authority is arguably somewhat extreme. Goffman described four candidate coping mechanisms, with the proviso that many inmates use a combination of them to get by. The first two, withdrawal and intransigence, become lifelong hallmarks of Lisbeth's posture in the world. Goffman explained that such self-protective mechanisms have costs in the institution: "staff may directly penalize inmates for such activity, citing sullenness or insolence explicitly as grounds for further punishment."[13] This, too, mirrors Lisbeth's experience. Punitive "treatments," such as confinement in the isolation cell and force-feeding of both medication and food, follow defiant gestures on Lisbeth's part, such as refusing to speak to Dr. Teleborian and rejecting medication. "Salander had rapidly come to the realization that an 'unruly and unmanageable patient' was equivalent to one who questioned Teleborian's reasoning and expertise."[14]

The events of Lisbeth's life following her release from St. Stefan's are marked by the stigma of having been there in the first place: she is dogged by her record of insanity. Her experiences in the institution—many of which can be understood as typical—forged the lonely, resilient, distrustful, and angry person she would become.

I Know You Are but What Am I?

In his book *Stigma*, Goffman pointed out how labels such as "mentally ill" affect the everyday interactions of stigmatized people. *Stigma* is originally a Greek term referring to "bodily signs designed to expose something unusual and bad about the moral status of the signifier. The signs were cut or burnt into the body and advertised that the bearer was a slave, a criminal, or a traitor—a blemished person, ritually polluted, to be avoided, especially in public places."[15] Bjurman's confessional tattoo is an almost-too-good example of this old meaning. Today, *stigma* refers "more to the disgrace itself than to the bodily evidence of it."[16] Someone is stigmatized if she is *perceived as* belonging to an undesirable category of person, whether she does or not.

Goffman identified three types of stigma: abominations or disfigurements of the body; blemishes of character such as a known record of mental disorder, criminality, unemployment, homosexuality, or alcoholism; and tribal stigmas of race, nation, and religion. Lisbeth's stigmatizing attributes seem to grow exponentially as the books unfold but belong mostly to the second category. Occasionally, her extremely small stature and her voluntary tattoos and piercings are read as examples of the first type, but she is routinely accused of mental and moral failings. According to Goffman, when we attribute a stigma to someone, we reduce the individual in our minds from "a whole and usual person to a tainted, discounted one," and thereby "exercise varieties of discrimination, through which we effectively, if often unthinkingly, reduce his life chances."[17]

Lisbeth "did not give a damn about labels," but they stuck to her like gooey Swedish fish.[18] The evidence of her mental illness, gathered from documentation of her time at St. Stefan's, looms large. When police first gather up her paper trail, the prosecutor Ekström describes her as "a woman who during her teens was in and out of psychiatric units, who is understood to make her living as a prostitute, who was declared incompetent by the district court, and who has been documented as having violent tendencies."[19] People assume that someone with one discreditable attribute is likely to have many. "We tend to impute a wide range of imperfections on the basis of the original one," Goffman wrote.[20] With little or no evidence, assumptions about promiscuity and violence become linked to mental illness. The slippery slope of stigma categories is demonstrated, with almost comical excess, when police and media are ready to believe and report any slanderous label leveled at Lisbeth, from "psychotic nutcase" to "lesbian Satanist."

Although she has countless enemies, Lisbeth is not without allies. Most notably, Dr. Palmgren, Dragan Armansky, Blomkvist, and Mimmi Wu find her almost endearing in her eccentricities. These friends fall into two different categories, both discussed by Goffman. First, Armansky and especially Palmgren are considered to be "wise." While they don't share the stigma with Lisbeth, the wise are "persons who are normal but whose special situation has made them intimately privy to the secret life of the stigmatized individual and sympathetic with it."[21] Palmgren, at least, is trusted enough to be let into Lisbeth's confidence, a rare privilege.

Blomkvist and Wu get to know Lisbeth under circumstances in which she is able to "pass" without their knowing of her flawed history. For someone discreditable, such as Lisbeth, hiding or otherwise managing prejudicial information is fraught with the constant risk of being found out. In a close relationship, this involves the double threat of being unmasked as flawed and of being accused of betrayal for hiding it in the first place. This fear prevents the stigmatized person from moving toward greater intimacy in relationships. For example, in *The Girl with the Dragon Tattoo*, Lisbeth considers potential sources of support after being brutally raped by Bjurman. She thinks first of her fellow band members:

> "Evil Fingers" would listen. They would also stand up for her. But they had no clue that Salander had a district court order declaring her non compos mentis. She didn't want them to be eyeing her the wrong way, too. *Not an option.*[22]

Managing a spoiled identity requires constant work and second-guessing: "to display or not to display; to tell or not to tell; to let on or not to let on; to lie or not to lie; and in each case, to whom, how, when, and where."[23]

Although she is an expert snoop into other people's business, Lisbeth is, understandably, intensely private. No wonder she has so few friends. Her social isolation, too, is characteristic of stigmatized individuals. Social interactions with people "in the know" can involve violence or simpering condescension. Like Lisbeth, many people with spoiled identities keep to themselves. Lacking the rewarding aspects of interpersonal contact, "the self-isolate can become suspicious, depressed, hostile, anxious, and bewildered."[24] Sounds like someone we know.

Girls, Interrupted

Long after her discharge from St. Stefan's at the age of fifteen, pages continue to be added to Lisbeth's incriminating casebook. This paper trail both prohibits her from "passing" in certain social situations and comes to play a dominant role in damning judgments made of her throughout the books.

Goffman described an ex–mental patient who avoided sharp exchanges with a spouse or an employer because a show of emotion might be taken as a sign of madness.[25] For stigmatized people, especially the so-called mentally ill, behavior that is even mildly confrontational validates their label and justifies further scrutiny and control. For the mercifully unlabeled, such behavior goes unnoticed.

This tendency is brought into stark and sometimes comical relief in Giannini's cross-examination of Dr. Teleborian in *The Girl Who Kicked the Hornet's Nest.* As evidence that Lisbeth represents a danger to herself, Dr. Teleborian cites her tattoos and piercings. They are, he testifies, a "manifestation of self-hate."[26] When Giannini asks whether she, too, is a danger to herself because of her earrings and a tattoo in a private place, Dr. Teleborian responds that tattoos can also be part of a social ritual. In this case, a so-called expert makes a determination that the same behavior demonstrated by one person is a symptom of illness, while for another it is an innocuous social performance. Although we can see the absurdity of this distinction when it is presented in this light, Goffman said that we do it all of the time in real life.

Teleborian walks into the same trap again and again during his testimony when he cites Lisbeth's "substance abuse" and "uncontrolled promiscuity" as evidence of her psychopathology. Because Lisbeth is already stigmatized, single instances of drunkenness are blown up into categorical labels. As Giannini points out, both she and Teleborian engaged in similar antics when they were young. "People do so many stupid things when they're seventeen," he replies.[27] Regular people do stupid things without consequence, while the serially scrutinized build up a self-incriminating biography.

Lest we think that this kind of thing happens only in fiction (or in Sweden), here is an example drawn from legal hearings under the Mental Health Act of Ontario, Canada. The purpose of the hearings is to review the involuntary commitment of patients, a status that requires a panel to affirm doctors' judgments that a patient is a danger to herself or others. In the first case, the patient was allegedly a danger to herself because she made "irrational" judgments about men.

> The clinical summary states that Ms. E.L. had been going to bars to pick up men she did not know and bringing them back to her apartment. Ms. E.L. told the panel that there was only one incident where she brought home a man she had just met. She said that she met a man she did not know outside a local library. It was cold and he offered her his jacket. They subsequently went out for coffee, following which Ms. E.L. invited the man to her apartment.[28]

This passage illustrates two moves that we've seen made in Lisbeth's case. First, the doctor generalized a single incident into a pattern. Second, the incident does not seem all that out of the ordinary: we would find it entirely believable in the context of a romantic comedy, for example. It is made to seem risky, though, when it is coupled with a prior diagnosis of mental illness and when it is presented by a medical authority in the stark setting of a hearing.

In a second such case, a doctor claimed that the patient's candle lighting constituted a danger to herself.[29] In both cases, there was no actual harm—no sexual assault or fire—but discredited individuals were being classified as dangerous "for their own good." Their possibilities for action—whether rational or risky—are clearly more constrained than those allowed an average person.

Lisbeth's story can be used as a lever to open a window on the social situation of stigmatized people more generally and particularly of those understood as "mentally ill." We agree that Lisbeth should be read as "one of us," but there may not be *any* "them." We want to challenge the practice of sorting people into dichotomous boxes: us/them, sane/insane, good/bad, and so on. Another way of saying this is that we are all "one of us," somewhere on the always-shifting continuum from sane to mad. We all suffer from spoiled identities at some point or another. "The most fortunate of normals is likely to have his half-hidden failing, and for every little failing there is a social occasion when it will loom large, creating a shameful gap" between how others see him and how he sees himself.[30] The conclusion is not that we should be nicer to people who are different from us, but that we should see ourselves in them and see them in ourselves. A mere slip of the pen, and our places could be reversed.

NOTES

1. Stieg Larsson, *The Girl Who Played with Fire*, trans. Reg Keeland (New York: Vintage, 2010), p. 47.

2. Ibid., pp. 319–320.

3. Stieg Larsson, *The Girl Who Kicked the Hornet's Nest*, trans. Reg Keeland (New York: Alfred A. Knopf, 2010), p. 484.

4. Goffman's insights are drawn from ethnographic methods, which include participant observation. For *Asylums*, he posed for a year as a recreation assistant at St. Elizabeth's Hospital in Washington, D.C.

5. Erving Goffman, *Asylums: Essays on the Social Situation of Mental Patients and Other Inmates* (New York: Anchor Books, 1961), p. 14.

6. Ibid., p. 16.

7. Ibid., p. 20.

8. Stieg Larsson, *The Girl with the Dragon Tattoo*, trans. Reg Keeland (New York: Vintage, 2009), p. 160.

9. Goffman, *Asylums*, pp. 153–154.

10. Ibid., p. 45.

11. Larsson, *The Girl Who Played with Fire*, p. 395.

12. Larsson, *The Girl Who Kicked the Hornet's Nest*, p. 497.

13. Goffman, *Asylums*, p. 36.

14. Larsson, *The Girl Who Played with Fire*, p. 393.

15. Erving Goffman, *Stigma: Notes on the Management of Spoiled Identity* (New York: Touchstone, 1986), p. 1.

16. Ibid., pp. 1–2.

17. Ibid., pp. 3, 5.

18. Larsson, *The Girl with the Dragon Tattoo*, p. 327.

19. Larsson, *The Girl Who Played with Fire*, p. 249.

20. Goffman, *Stigma*, p. 5.

21. Ibid., p. 28.

22. Larsson, *The Girl with the Dragon Tattoo*, p. 237.

23. Goffman, *Stigma*, p. 42.

24. Ibid., p. 13.

25. Ibid., p. 15.

26. Larsson, *The Girl Who Kicked the Hornet's Nest*, p. 487.

27. Ibid., p. 500.

28. Re C.C., [2005] O.C.C.B.D., No. 178 (O.C.C.B.), online: QL (OCCBD).

29. Re C.C., [2004] O.C.C.B.D., No. 62 (O.C.C.B.), online: QL (OCCBD).

30. Goffman, *Stigma*, p. 127.

THE *MIS*-EDUCATION OF LISBETH SALANDER AND THE ALCHEMY OF THE AT-RISK CHILD

Chad William Timm

With regard to her personal record, the opinion concluded that there was a *grave risk of alcohol and drug abuse,* and that she *lacked self-awareness.* By then her casebook was filled with terms such as *introverted, socially inhibited, lacking in empathy, ego-fixated, psychopathic and asocial behavior, difficulty in cooperating,* and *incapable of assimilating learning.* Anyone who read her casebook might be tempted to conclude that Salander was seriously retarded.[1]

Based on this evaluation by the assistant head of the social welfare board, it's not surprising that Lisbeth "the Idiot" Salander failed to earn a high school diploma or even a certificate that she could read and write. In every way Lisbeth did not demonstrate academic competency, consistently failing to display mastery of the essential skills and concepts deemed valuable by school officials. She wasn't only labeled an idiot; she was *at grave risk* of failure in both school and life. And yet based on the evaluations of those who know her best, Mikael Blomkvist, Dragan Armansky, and Holger Palmgren, Lisbeth is nothing less than brilliant. Her idea of relaxation, for example, includes reading highly sophisticated scholarly texts such as *Spirals—Mysteries of DNA*, a brick of a book filled with the most current DNA research. Dr. Jonasson, who gives the book to Lisbeth as a gift, tells her, "Someday I'd be interested to hear how it is that you can read academic texts that even I can't understand."[2]

How is it that a young woman deemed at risk of every possible social malady imaginable and labeled "retarded" can solve incredibly sophisticated mathematic, scientific, and computer-related problems? How does a seemingly brilliant girl such as Lisbeth fall through the cracks of an educational system? How do schools know the difference between a problem-solving child and one who is at risk of academic failure? The French philosopher Michel Foucault (1926–1984) can help us answer these questions by analyzing the ways school officials use their positions of power to separate and categorize students such as Lisbeth, essentially constructing their identities.

Knowledge Is Power

Foucault famously investigated the manner in which the "art of government" evolved in Europe between the sixteenth and eighteenth centuries to include less outwardly violent forms of control.[3] By analyzing the prison, the hospital, the insane asylum, and the school, Foucault exposed ways in which these institutions defined knowledge and then classified the criminal, the sick, or the insane. The purpose of "knowing" and classifying criminals justified their imprisonment and taught them to know themselves as deviant.

Authorities, for example, operating on behalf of the government or with institutional support, identified certain desired qualities and characteristics and then sorted people into categories. Imagine your first-grade teacher sorting the fast readers into a group called "hares" and the slow readers into a group called "tortoises." Foucault contended that this kind of sorting takes place "because knowledge is not made for understanding; it is made for cutting."[4] By sorting people into categories such as criminal, deviant, insane, or intelligent, those doing the cutting and sorting gain a tremendous amount of power in the form of knowledge. According to Foucault, "Power produces; it produces reality; it produces domains of objects and rituals of truth."[5] This knowledge-power paradigm allows the authorities to continue determining what characteristics to classify and sort.[6]

The sophisticated interplay between knowledge and power is especially relevant to a formal educational environment. Lisbeth had no academic success in a traditional school environment, to the point that her teachers "ignored her and allowed her to sit in sullen silence."[7] Instead of recognizing her unique brilliance, school officials labeled her a failure. Although Lisbeth's schooling took place in Sweden, I will use the recent standards and accountability movement in the United States as a backdrop. The objectives of the movement fostered the creation of an environment of discipline and surveillance that made the construction of the at-risk child all the more likely.

No Child Left Unharmed

In recent years, the outcry for public school reform has led the federal government to take unprecedented steps to regulate schooling in the United States. Consequently, federal legislation now mandates standards and accountability. Standards refer to what children are taught in school and how well they demonstrate their knowledge, with an emphasis on reading, math, and science. Accountability refers to the consequences schools face when students do not demonstrate proficiency with the standards. The bastard child of the standards and accountability movement was President George W. Bush's 2002 No Child Left Behind Act (NCLB), recently renamed by President Barack Obama as the Race to the Top Program. According to NCLB, a student is proficient if his or her score on a standardized test places the student within a certain percentile rank, generally above the 40th percentile, and a school is successful if students demonstrate "adequate yearly progress" toward the goal of 100 percent proficiency. Yes, you read correctly: the initial bill required 100 percent proficiency by 2014, which, of course, is statistically impossible!

In order to determine whether a school is meeting annual yearly progress, policy makers determine what a successful student looks like. In terms of the current educational reform movement, a successful student is one who demonstrates proficiency on a standardized test. Thus, NCLB requires educators to define a problem solver as one who solves problems in a prescribed manner, at a prescribed time, in a prescribed location. Educational philosopher Thomas Popkewitz uses Foucault to analyze how this educational policy constructs students as "problem solvers," a process he fittingly calls a kind of "alchemy." Because students are not mathematicians, scientists, or historians, academic knowledge must be adapted to schooling through teaching strategies. In order to know whether a student is "getting it," educational experts identify certain student actions or ways of thinking that sufficiently reflect mastery. This process then results in "fabricating the problem-solving child as a particular human kind for pedagogical intervention."[8] In this way, teaching is not really about mathematics, science, or history but instead a process whereby students' thoughts and actions are normalized and mapped. As a result of this mapping, students who can solve problems in the prescribed manner are labeled "problem solvers" and those who cannot are labeled "at risk" of academic failure.

The child as a problem solver is a particular human kind, as is the at-risk child. Schools subjectively create lists of qualities and characteristics of these human kinds, use the lists to identify students who meet the criteria, and then act on the children in ways designed to encourage problem solving and to discourage at-risk behaviors. Thus, these human kinds are actually fabrications; after all, how can we know what a problem solver or a student at risk is if we don't establish parameters to use in identifying them? Furthermore, identifying the problem-solving child simultaneously produces the exact opposite, the disadvantaged child who cannot solve problems and is therefore at risk of failure. Multiple choice, fill-in-the-bubble exams require students to think in certain limited ways, and teachers are forced to teach to those understandings so that students are proficient and their schools don't lose funding. Thus, when students don't show understanding by scoring high enough on the tests or by regurgitating the teacher's words back to him or her, they're determined to be at risk of academic failure.

Wannabe Swedes can imagine the educational expert as Odin, the Norse god of wisdom and logic, flanked by his two ravens, Hugin and Munin. Odin waves his staff and sends Hugin with "content knowledge" and Munin with "qualities of the proficient student" to the four corners of the world, thus producing the perfect problem-solving child.[9] Now that's a creepy thought.

Intellectual Gifts

Lisbeth Salander didn't demonstrate problem solving in ways deemed acceptable by her teachers. In the schools Lisbeth attended, the "problem-solving" student politely answered questions when asked. Lisbeth, on the other hand, quite often refused to even speak in school. As described in *The Girl with the Dragon Tattoo*:

> She had never been particularly talkative, and she became known as the pupil who never raised her hand and often did not answer when a teacher asked her a direct question. No-one was sure whether this was because she did not know the answer or if there was some other reason, which was reflected in her grades.[10]

Because of her unwillingness to answer questions and demonstrate acceptable problem-solving abilities, "She also aroused very little sympathy among the teachers."[11] Although Lisbeth's refusal to answer questions led her teachers to give up on her and caused her grades to suffer, it's not proof that she didn't demonstrate knowledge of the subject matter. After all, her experiences with question-and-answer time in the classroom weren't necessarily positive. We know that on one occasion when Lisbeth was eleven, she was questioned by substitute math teacher Birgitta Miaas, "who time after time had tried to get her [Lisbeth] to answer a question that she'd already answered correctly, even though the answer key in the textbook said she was wrong. In fact, the textbook was wrong and as far as Salander was concerned that should be obvious to everyone."[12] The outcome of this situation led Miaas to grab Salander's shoulder and Lisbeth to throw a book at Miaas's head. This was not the only time Lisbeth showed she could indeed solve problems and display brilliance. For example, Lisbeth could solve puzzles and riddles from a very young age, such as when her mother gave her a Rubik's cube at age nine. "It had put her abilities to the test for barely forty frustrating minutes before she understood how it worked."[13] We learn that in elementary school, she consistently solved the daily newspaper's intelligence tests and knew how to add and subtract and that "Multiplication, division, and geometry were a natural extension."[14] If any label should be applied to Lisbeth, it would be "gifted and talented." Yet because she couldn't solve problems within the rigid definition of the school, "She completed the nine years of compulsory schooling without a certificate."[15]

Even though Lisbeth failed in this type of traditional school setting, her failure in no way reflected her problem-solving ability. Blomkvist remarks that "her intellectual gifts are undeniable."[16] Indeed, Lisbeth uses her great talents as a computer hacker to help Erika Berger solve her pervert problem and identify Peter Fredriksson as a stalker. Not only can Lisbeth solve problems, she also understands the nature of mathematical problems in a way that few people in the world can. Lisbeth comes to understand that "Mathematics was actually a logic puzzle with endless variations—riddles that could be solved. The trick was not to solve arithmetical problems. . . . The trick was to understand combinations of the various rules that made it possible to solve any mathematical problem whatsoever."[17] Indeed, her mathematical epiphany allows her to eventually grapple with the theorem of mathematical giant Pierre de Fermat, a problem that had stumped the world's leading mathematicians for hundreds of years.

The fact that Lisbeth can solve problems, just not when, where, and how school officials expected her to, demonstrates the alchemy with which the problem-solving child is created. Lisbeth is knowledgeable, though not knowledgeable in the narrow and limited way that schools determine knowledge in the twenty-first century. Naming or creating the problem-solving or knowledgeable child and, indirectly, the at-risk child serves a dual purpose, as Foucault described, "That of binary division and branding (mad/sane; dangerous/harmless; normal/abnormal) . . . [and] how a constant surveillance is to be exercised over him in an individual way."[18]

This process of binary division and branding allows school officials to identify and categorize students in order to act on them. It also encourages children to act on themselves.

In a sense, the alchemy of naming the at-risk student etches this new identity into the very being of the child, just as the tattoo artist permanently embedded the ink of the dragon tattoo into Lisbeth's skin, only deeper into the soul. The result is a child who sees herself as at risk. Furthermore, when children are labeled at risk, they are put under constant surveillance; everything they do is watched closely. The school experts claim this surveillance is for the children's own good, to reduce their risk of failure, but they also want to carefully control and police behaviors in ways that encourage children to toe the line.

Panoptic Power

Once the process of separation and categorization is complete and a particular identity is named, disciplinary power also acts to encourage the "named" to govern themselves. Perhaps Foucault's most well-known example of this aspect of disciplinary power is his analysis of the Panopticon, a new kind of prison conceived by the British philosopher Jeremy Bentham (1748–1832). The architectural design for the Panopticon called for a prison, circular in shape, with numerous levels filled with cells. Each cell faced the interior of the prison, where a tall guard tower stood in the center of a courtyard, as if it were the hub of a giant wheel, visible from the door of each cell. Each cell had two windows: one small window facing the outside of the prison, and one larger facing the guard tower. Describing the guard tower, Foucault said, "By the effect of backlighting, one can observe from the tower, standing out precisely against the light, the small captive shadows in the cells of the periphery. They are like so many cages, so many small theatres, in which each actor is alone, perfectly individualized and constantly visible."[19]

According to Foucault, "In order to make the presence or absence of the inspector unverifiable, so that the prisoners, in their cells, cannot even see a shadow, Bentham envisaged . . . venetian blinds on the windows of the central observation hall."[20] Thus, the Panopticon was structured in a way that allowed the guard in the tower to observe the actions of the prisoners at all times, but the prisoners could not observe other inmates or the guard. Consequently, the inmate believed he was always being watched but never knew whether he actually was. The prisoner, never sure if his actions were under surveillance, began to act upon the belief that the observation was constant. Foucault wrote, "Hence the major effect of the Panopticon: to induce in the inmate a state of conscious and permanent visibility that assures the automatic functioning of power."[21] Prison officials would rarely need to take corrective action because prisoners would take action themselves. They would behave as they were expected to because they would believe they were being watched; in effect, they would construct new identities as behaving inmates. For the legal system, once the qualities and the characteristics of the criminal or the insane were identified, subjects fitting those criteria could be apprehended, categorized, and incarcerated. Incarceration in the Panopticon would then teach criminals to identify themselves as deviant and to begin the process of self-regulation.

Teach . . . Your Children Well

The disciplinary power that schools employ by separating and categorizing students has a similar panoptic effect. When a child is identified as unable to solve problems and is therefore labeled at risk of academic failure, school officials have carte blanche to scrutinize and regulate all behavior. This is especially true in the U.S. educational system, because the potential factors that place children at risk of academic failure are defined broadly. According to the U.S. Census Bureau, the following conditions may place a child at risk of failure: neither parent or guardian is employed, has a family income of less than $10,000, either parent immigrated in the last five years, does not live with both parents, speaks English less than "very well," retained in a grade at least once, or has at least one disability.[22] Because so many factors contribute to placing a child at risk, the school is allowed to act on every type of student behavior and claim that the purpose is to reduce risk. Schools, therefore, have an incredibly powerful tool at their disposal: the power to categorize students as at risk, and the ability to discipline at-risk students when necessary.

For example, if a teacher knows a child is at risk due to the fact that the student comes from a low-income home, she can try to regulate all of the student's behaviors in order to lessen the risk factor. In this respect, the identification of a student as at risk becomes a self-fulfilling prophecy: because the student is treated as if he is unable to solve problems and is at risk of failure, he begins to see himself as a failure and acts accordingly.

We see evidence of this panoptic influence in schooling in Lisbeth's experiences. Because Lisbeth didn't fit the criteria for being a problem-solving child, all of her other qualities and characteristics were opened up for scrutiny. The fact that she was quiet and reserved was scrutinized and became a problem: "She minded her own business and didn't interfere with what anyone around her did. Yet there was always someone who absolutely would not leave her in peace."[23] Her inability to interact with other students in socially acceptable ways became an issue. On two specific occasions, she fought with other students, much larger boys. On both of these occasions, the boys had bullied Lisbeth, and she fought back in self-defense. As her attorney Annika Giannini describes, "I can go back to her school records and examine one situation after another in which Lisbeth turned violent. The incidents were always preceded by some kind of provocation. I can easily recognize the signs of bullying."[24] Because Lisbeth had already been deemed at risk, her identity as a girl who was unable to solve problems either academically or socially became fixed, and it was assumed that she herself was the cause of all of these problems.

Lisbeth was also encouraged to act on herself in a panoptic fashion. First, she was imprisoned at St. Stefan's, where she was put under constant surveillance and strapped to a bed for 381 consecutive days. On her thirteenth birthday, "She must have dozed off, because she did not hear the footsteps, but she was wide awake when the door opened. The light from the doorway blinded her. . . . He stood at the foot of her bed and observed her for a long time. . . . She could see him only in silhouette from the light in the doorway."[25] This example of the powerful Dr. Teleborian observing Lisbeth is eerily similar to Foucault's description of the guard tower in the Panopticon. Lisbeth is constantly under surveillance and the gaze of her captor is incessant, but she cannot always see him. Then, on being released from St. Stefan's her surveillance continues as she is put under legal guardianship. Lisbeth's guardians, first Holger Palmgren and then the rapist pig Nils Bjurman, keep close tabs on her. How much money she has access to and spends is regulated, her alcohol consumption is prohibited, and she's always being watched, her every action scrutinized. Beginning in school, she is identified as possessing certain characteristics, she is sorted, she is acted on, and then she is encouraged to act on and punish herself. According to Foucault, "In its function, the power to punish is not necessarily different from that of curing or educating."[26]

I Don't Wanna Be Learned!

So, was Lisbeth really at risk of academic failure? Of course, she was! Her father was a former Soviet spy who brutally beat her mother. Did this place her at risk of academic failure? Absolutely! Did it impact her ability to interact with others? Of course it did! So what's the point?

When a person encounters Foucault for the first time, it's easy to feel paralyzed, like Lisbeth lying in the hospital with her hands strapped to the bed, unable to move even the slightest bit. Foucault so meticulously demonstrated how all relations are reducible to power that people cannot act without considering how they are wielding power or how power is being wielded over them. Yet according to Foucault, his "point is not that everything is bad, but that everything is dangerous, which is not the same as bad. If everything is dangerous then we always have something to do."[27] Reading Foucault in light of his claim that power is dangerous fosters a sense of hyper-awareness and activism that compels us to identify when power is being abused.

All power is potentially dangerous. So it's not that we shouldn't identify the problem-solving or at-risk child, but that we should always critique the manner in which we define her and take into consideration what impact the categorization will have on the child. In the case of Lisbeth Salander, the results were devastating. Instead of using the knowledge that Lisbeth didn't solve problems in a conventional manner to help her succeed, her teachers used this knowledge to excuse their failure to teach her, ignore her cries for help, and try to control every aspect of her life in order to coerce her into conformity. On a much broader scale, this is exactly what No Child Left Behind sought to do to schools across the country. The accountability mandated by the law works to discipline and "normalize" schools so that they aren't substantially different from one another. A school falling outside of what is deemed acceptable, or "normal" in terms of the percentage of students achieving proficiency, is subject to surveillance, discipline, and punishment. Schools then pass the discipline, punishment, and surveillance on to their students.

We can, however, resist the alchemy of the at-risk child. By recognizing that these categories are socially constructed and not universal truths, we can overturn them; we can reverse the panoptic effects of education. We *can* reenvision ways to determine school success in a less oppressive manner.

Still, the alchemy of education is perpetual. Schooling is full of games of truth where teachers are constantly defining and redefining what it means to be a successful, well-adjusted, knowledgeable student in each of their classrooms. Foucault claimed, "The problem in such practices where power—which is not in itself a bad thing—must inevitably come into play is knowing how to avoid the kind of domination effects where a kid is subjected to the arbitrary and unnecessary authority of a teacher, or a student put under the thumb of a professor who abuses his authority."[28] Lisbeth Salander, like thousands of American students, found herself under the thumb of her teachers, her therapists, and her guardians. Instead of succumbing to the power of her teachers, Lisbeth resisted. Her refusal to be disciplined or to discipline herself in the way her teachers wanted her to eventually guaranteed her failure in school. This resistance, eventually taking the form of tattoos, piercings, leather, and a violently asocial attitude, further justified her at-risk label later in life. If, despite years of *mis*-education, Lisbeth Salander could still solve some of the most complicated mathematical problems in existence, imagine what she could have done in an educational system that resisted labeling her and instead gave her the freedom to learn in her own way.

NOTES

1. Stieg Larsson, *The Girl with the Dragon Tattoo*, trans. Reg Keeland (New York: Vintage, 2009), p. 160.

2. Stieg Larsson, *The Girl Who Kicked the Hornet's Nest*, trans. Reg Keeland (New York: Alfred A. Knopf, 2010), p. 390.

3. Michel Foucault, *Discipline and Punish: The Birth of the Prison*, trans. Alan Sheridan (New York: Vintage Press, 1995).

4. Michel Foucault, "Nietzsche, Genealogy, History," in P. Rabinow and N. Rose, eds., *The Essential Foucault: Selections from the Essential Works of Foucault, 1954–1984* (New York: New Press, 2003), p. 360.

5. Foucault, "'Omnes Et Singulatim': Toward a Critique of Political Reason," in *The Essential Foucault*, p. 194.

6. See Aryn Martin and Mary Simms's chapter in this book, "Labeling Lisbeth: Sti(e)gma and Spoiled Identity."

7. Larsson, *The Girl with the Dragon Tattoo*, p. 230.

8. Thomas Popkewitz, "The Alchemy of the Mathematics Curriculum: Inscriptions and the Fabrication of the Child," *American Educational Research Journal* 41, no. 1 (2004): 3–34.

9. Odin was also the god of warfare, battle, and death. For more on Odin, see John Lindow, *Norse Mythology: A Guide to Gods, Heroes, Rituals, and Beliefs* (New York: Oxford University Press, 2002).

10. Larsson, *The Girl with the Dragon Tattoo*, pp. 229–230.

11. Ibid., p. 229.

12. Stieg Larsson, *The Girl Who Played with Fire*, trans. Reg Keeland (New York: Vintage, 2010), p. 391.

13. Ibid., p. 23.

14. Ibid., p. 24.

15. Larsson, *The Girl with the Dragon Tattoo*, p. 158.

16. Larsson, *The Girl Who Kicked the Hornet's Nest*, p. 50.

17. Larsson, *The Girl Who Played with Fire*, p. 24.

18. Foucault, *Discipline and Punish*, p. 199.

19. Ibid., p. 200.

20. Ibid., p. 201.

21. Ibid.

22. Kominsky, Jameson, and Martinez, U.S. Census Bureau.

23. Larsson, *The Girl with the Dragon Tattoo*, pp. 228–229.

24. Larsson, *The Girl Who Kicked the Hornet's Nest*, p. 502.

25. Larsson, *The Girl Who Played with Fire*, pp. 4–5.

26. Foucault, *Discipline and Punish*, p. 303.

27. Michel Foucault, "On the Genealogy of Ethics: An Overview of Work in Progress," in *The Essential Foucault*, p. 104.

28. Michel Foucault, "The Ethics of the Concern of the Self as a Practice of Freedom," in *The Essential Foucault*, p. 40.

THE GIRL WHO TURNED THE TABLES: A QUEER READING OF LISBETH SALANDER

Kim Surkan

The runaway success of Stieg Larsson's *Millennium Trilogy* has been all the more surprising given the unconventional portrayal of Lisbeth Salander, an abuse survivor who is anything but a stereotypical crime fiction victim and perhaps an even more unlikely private investigator. Pierced and tattooed, Salander is a highly intelligent but antisocial computer hacker with a profound distrust of authority and a propensity for violence. In *The Girl Who Played with Fire*, a coworker tells us that she "wasn't exactly a person you warmed to."[1] Yet it is precisely her deviance, her radical resistance to societal and sexual norms, that makes her (and the series) compelling. In three novels centrally framed around misogyny and violence against women, the bisexual, punk Salander overtly rejects conventional notions of gender and sexual identity in such a way as to call into question basic assumptions about gendered power relations in society.[2]

But is she a feminist character or an apolitical, androgynous, queer iconoclast? The debate on this question points to the critical schism between feminist and queer readings, as well as to the strategic ambiguity of Salander as a character.[3] Reading Salander as "genderqueer," rather than as woman, allows us to understand her as a hybrid of these two positions (queer and feminist) by situating her in a feminist framework as a character with a unique relationship to sexual power and gendered violence.[4] Lisbeth represents many of the contradictions and promises of contemporary gender theory and enables a more complex understanding of feminist and radical sexual politics. Ultimately, Salander's feminism lies in her swift and consistent (albeit unconventionally violent) retaliation against those who abuse women, as well as in her economic and sexual independence from men. The murkier question of her relationship to specific identity positions—such as "woman," "feminist," "lesbian," "genderqueer," or even "queer"—make her all the more controversial, particularly given her own ambivalence about claiming such labels.

The historical rift between feminist and queer political thought (and, more recently, between some types of feminism and transgender politics) may well return to a discussion of gender essentialism and the political problem for feminists in formulating "woman" as a coherent identity category. As Linda Martin Alcoff wrote, "the dilemma facing feminist theorists today is that our very self-definition is grounded in a concept that we must deconstruct and de-essentialize in all of its aspects."[5] Earlier feminists of the 1960s and 1970s took a much less complicated political stance. "They viewed sexism as a straightforward matter of women being oppressed at the hands of men."[6] In most cases, the understanding of those two gender categories, "women" and "men," were not problematized in the 1960s and 1970s—and, as Julia Serano points out, femininity was perceived as a coercive "program that was seen as inherently stifling and which fostered (or was the product of) women's subservience and subjugation to men."[7] So while these earlier feminists might have applauded Salander's rejection of conventional femininity, her decision to get breast implants in *The Girl Who Played with Fire* and her resistance to labels of any kind complicate her relationship to a simple identity of womanhood. Rather, Lisbeth figures as a more complex, deconstructionist character whose defiance of norms and gender roles keeps troubling our reading of her both as "woman" and as a feminist.

Queer theory sidesteps the specificity of gender in its replacement of *gay* and *lesbian* with the gender-nonspecific term *queer*. As Annamarie Jagose explains, queer "may better be understood as promoting a non-identity—or even anti-identity—politics."[8] Salander's disregard for any affiliation with a particular sexual identity would therefore not be at odds with a queer politic, even though she herself would not necessarily self-identify with that term. Furthermore, her unconventional gender expression and appropriation of male power and masculine privilege through the use of information technology and hacking skills invite a consideration of Salander as a specifically genderqueer protagonist.

"I Am Also an Alien": The Girl Who Was Not One

In Lisbeth Salander, Larsson has succeeded in creating a character with feminist values who resists a feminism based on identity politics, as she defies all of the stereotypes of femininity associated with conventional womanhood. In fact, she is a "girl" who in many ways is not one at all. Salander is represented as highly androgynous, described initially by her boss Dragan Armansky as "a pale, anorexic young woman who had hair as short as a fuse, and a pierced nose and eyebrows."[9] Despite his avowal that "he was not interested in flat-chested girls who might be mistaken for skinny boys at a distance," he finds himself attracted to her.[10] The irreverent Goth/punk Salander is decidedly genderqueer; her occupation of the border zone between man and woman destabilizes the normalized heterosexuality of men such as Armansky who desire her, and by implication she "queers" Larsson's readers as well.

In addition, Larsson describes Lisbeth as someone with a strong personal moral code and a vengeful nature, but not as a person with overtly stated political beliefs. Her propensity for violence, for example, is not indiscriminately or specifically directed at men, but rather, in the words of her guardian Holger Palmgren, against those who would do her harm: "If she's provoked or threatened, she can strike back with appalling violence."[11] As critic Jenni Miller wrote, "While Salander was written to be and has been embraced as a feminist heroine, she herself would probably not give a crap either way as long as everyone would just leave her alone, already."[12] Miller further takes issue with the description of Salander as a "violent femme," describing her as androgynous and writing that "she's not femme at all," pointing to her tattoos, masculine attire, membership in the hacker community, and aggressive sexuality as evidence.

Androgyny on the female body translates into a perception of butchness or masculinity:

> Man is the universal. Woman is defined by her opposition to man, by what she does not have, the Penis, and the one thing she has that man does not, reproduction and sexuality. Thus, to be androgynous is not to be gender-neutral, but male. . . . In a culture centered on Man, Woman will always be the genderqueer. This has made woman an inherently fragile project.[13]

Taken together, Salander's body modifications and wardrobe "undo" any possibility of reading her as conventionally gendered and cast doubt on her sex as well, despite her small stature (under five feet tall).

The distinction between sex and gender is important for the definition of genderqueer and our understanding of Salander. As feminist philosopher Judith Butler points out, "When the constructed status of gender is theorized as radically independent of sex, gender itself becomes a free-floating artifice, with the consequence that *man* and *masculine* might just as easily signify a female body as a male one, and *woman* and *feminine* a male body as easily as a female one."[14] So the genderqueer subject is one whose body does not match the conventions of culturally assigned gender associated with a particular sex. Salander, anatomically female, is anything but feminine, exhibiting what Judith Halberstam has termed "female masculinity" in her gender presentation and actions.[15]

The Masculinity of Violence

Noomi Rapace, the actress who played Salander in the Swedish film adaptations of the three novels, says that to prepare for the role she "wanted to be more like a boy, a bit more masculine," and consequently lost weight "to get rid of my female softness," learned kickboxing, cut her hair, pierced herself, and got a motorcycle license.[16] In an interview, Rapace points to Salander's rejection of victimization as the source of her appeal to women in particular: "She does not complain and she doesn't accept being a victim. Almost everybody has treated her so badly and has done horrible things to her but she doesn't accept it and won't become the victim they have tried to force her to be."[17]

Salander's aversion to being cast as a victim—which she expresses through revenge and violence—can also be seen in her resistance to conventional femininity. To be read as a feminine female is to be subject to harassment, stalking, violence, and rape at the hands of men, because, as Michael Kimmel observes, the "chief building block in the social construction of sexuality is gender. . . . The difference between male and female sexuality reproduces men's power over women."[18] Salander's embodied genderqueerness is a rejection of that power dynamic, as is her tendency to resort to violence in the face of sexual threats.

Salander herself does not demonstrate feminist conscious-ness in a political sense about sexual violence, which she sees as the inevitable status quo for women or, at least, women of a certain social class. "By the time she was eighteen, Salander did not know a single girl who at some point had not been forced to perform some sort of sexual act against her will. . . . In her world, this was the natural order of things. As a girl she was legal prey, especially if she was dressed in a worn black leather jacket and had pierced eyebrows, tattoos, and zero social status."[19] Her viewpoint is strictly pragmatic: "there was no point whimpering about it," and therefore she doesn't stop to ponder the sociological reasons for rape or engage in philosophical discussions about feminist projects for change. Her vigilante response to sexual violence is the response of an individual who has been wronged, rather than of a crusader on behalf of a social class. Still, Larsson complicates our read-ing of Salander by placing her story within the framework of a series of Swedish crime statistics about sexual violence against women. Although she wouldn't deign to approach authorities herself as recourse for her own rape, she is clearly aware of the existence of feminist social services because she donates her meager inheritance from her mother to "one of Stockholm's crisis centres for women."[20]

Perhaps much of the dispute about whether to interpret Salander as a feminist heroine is actually the result of gen-der confusion or, as Judith Butler would have it, "gender trouble."[21] Readers struggle to reconcile Lisbeth's androgynous appearance, unconventional sexuality, and violent tenden-cies with her membership in the category "woman." Salander is an exceedingly "queer" figure; her difference from others is so profound that even her mental competence is called into question—and much of that difference is made visible in her failure to conform to gender norms. The paradox of Salander's feminism is that it hinges precisely on the extent to which she is understood as a woman and therefore the degree to which we perceive her as a normal female beset by sexism and gender-based violence. If her penetrative violence against male aggressors (which includes firebombing her father, raping and tattooing Bjurman, shooting Lundin, and nail-gunning Niederman) is taken as evidence of her depravity, rather than as a measured (if extreme) response to violence against women in the context of an unjust society, then the political impact of her actions as feminist is called into question. But such violence, coded masculine, will always be seen as madness when enacted by a female, because feminine women would never do these things.

"I Can Be a Regular Bitch. Just Try Me"

Ultimately, Salander's gender identity is a composite of her outward appearance and her behavior. As Judith Butler defines it, gender is performative.[22] Although it has the appearance of being "natural," gender is always and continuously constructed.

Larsson has been roundly criticized by feminists for Salander's decision to get a breast augmentation. At first glance, this would seem to be a plot twist that wholly contradicts a reading of her as genderqueer and perhaps even as feminist, because breast implants are often viewed as objectifying the female body for men's pleasure. But Salander's surgery is cast as a medical solution to an abnormality. "Her own doctor, a charmingly hard-boiled woman named Alessandra Perrini, had told her that her breasts were abnormally underdeveloped, and that the enlargement could therefore be performed for medical reasons."[23] Larsson invites us to read her surgery as a form of sex reassignment, strategically engineered to edge her closer to a normatively feminine appearance in congruence with her female sex.

If Larsson is attempting to correlate Salander's realization of some measure of femininity with a coming-of-age theme (as he seems to do in her musings when she considers herself in the mirror in *The Girl Who Played with Fire*), he has misunderstood the power and appeal of his character as a genderqueer subject.[24] Larsson suggests that Salander is biologically deficient as a female—she is very thin and is described as having "child-like breasts," which she sees as "pathetic," prompting her to get implants. This has two effects: it presents her as "naturally" androgynous (masculine) and suggests that she is more comfortable in a normatively gendered body. Salander's breast augmentation can instead be seen as simply the latest in a series of body modifications that impact her gender presentation, rather than the defining surgery that restores her sense of femininity. In Salander's case, the queerness of her gender (and sexuality) and the indeterminate features of her "sexed" body undermine the normalizing effect of her breast implants.

Salander's gender presentation shifts dramatically during the course of the trilogy. She further alters her appearance to look more normal by removing a tattoo and several piercings, growing out her hair, and dressing more conservatively. Notice that these actions coincide with a dramatic (and illicit) shift in her class status. Her ability to first steal Wennerström's money and then to pass as a woman of means requires a level of gender normativity that renders her incognito.

It is precisely through such actions, however, that the performance of gender is demonstrated in Larsson's fiction. Salander dresses in drag when she dons the respective personas of the "big-busted heiress" Monica Sholes and the less ostentatious Irene Nesser. Both are constructed alias identities; she uses Sholes initially to fraudulently wire Wennerström's money from his accounts in the Cayman Islands, and Nesser subsequently becomes her means of evading authorities as a fugitive.

The success of her performances as Sholes and Nesser relies on their absolute adherence to "heteronormativity" and conventional femininity, providing a sharp contrast to the sexual and gender ambiguity displayed by Salander as she is portrayed in the rest of the trilogy.

"You Have the Right to Remain Silent"

Salander's experience is uncannily parallel to the history of sexuality that Michel Foucault (1926–1984) described in relationship to queer experience and the construction of queer identity.[25] Lisbeth is pathologized as deviant and is institutionalized, dominated, and contained, and her freedom is regulated, common experiences historically for those who transgressed sexual and gender norms.[26]

Salander's gender ambiguity is a phenomenon Foucault pointed to in his discussion of the "medicalization of the sexually peculiar," which he described as the discursive interplay of pleasure and power.[27] The pleasure of reading about her is fueled all the more by the reversals of sexual power that occur through her identity as hacker. Salander turns the tables on her victimization, using technology to penetrate, surveil, and expose the perversion of the very authorities who pathologized her. Her membership in the hacker community situates her firmly within a masculine social group with Bob the Dog. And her ability to enter the private sphere of another's e-mail account or hard drive is experienced as a violation, a metaphorical indicator of her aggressive sexuality—as Blomkvist is shocked to discover. *"You've been in my computer, Fröken Salander,"* he says aloud. *"You're a fucking hacker."*[28]

As a genderqueer subject, Salander is marked by reversals of gendered expectations regarding her sexuality—she is the instigator and the aggressor in her relationships with men but allows herself to be dominated by Mimmi in the one lesbian relationship portrayed in the trilogy. Object choice is far less important to her than the fulfillment of her sexual needs in an encounter, and again she proves to be surprisingly apolitical in her identity affiliation:

> Salander—unlike Mimmi—had never thought of herself as a lesbian. She had never brooded over whether she was straight, gay, or even bisexual. She did not give a damn about labels, did not see that it was anyone else's business whom she spent her nights with.[29]

In effect, Salander is driven by her libido to seduce and proposition prospective sexual partners, placing her in a traditionally masculine role, as when she seduces the boy in Grenada at the beginning of the second book. Despite this, Larsson characterizes her as "a quite normal woman, with the same desires and sex drive as every other woman."[30] Such a description would seem to speak more to the "normalcy" of women *having* desire, rather than to sexual orientation. In a discussion with Mimmi, however, Salander embraces her own sexual ambiguity:

> "Apart from the fact that you're not really a dyke. You're probably bisexual. But most of all you're sexual—you like sex and you don't care about what gender. You're an entropic chaos factor."
> "I don't know what I am," Salander said.[31]

Salander's silence and consistent refusal to speak to medical or other authorities are strategic forms of resistance. As Dr. Jonasson, the trauma physician treating the gunshot wound of the adult Salander, later observes, the forensic report on his patient "contains no diagnosis. It almost seems to be an academic study of a patient who refuses to speak."[32] Jonasson suggests that rather than being a sociopath, she may instead have Asperger's syndrome or another form of autism.[33]

In the absence of any concrete diagnosis of mental illness for Salander, her social and sexual deviance becomes the "truth" of her identity. Salander's act of violence against her father is taken as evidence of gender deviance; it is not behavior typical of a twelve-year-old girl. Compelled by her guardian (and later rapist) Nils Bjurman to detail her sexual history, she gives him "brief, colourless answers of the sort she assumed would fit with her psychological profile."[34]

If she understands her own gender presentation as a predisposition to becoming a victim of sexual violence, however, it doesn't prompt her to seek recourse within the justice system after being assaulted by her guardian. As Larsson described it, "Salander was not like any normal person. . . . [Filing] a report against Nils Bjurman for sexual assault did not even cross her mind."[35] Instead, she takes matters into her own hands, ultimately taking control of the discourse by physically marking him with the tattoo I AM A SADISTIC PIG, A PERVERT AND A RAPIST as a reminder of her power over him and perhaps also as a warning to other women.[36]

Sexuality and Representation

In his graphic portrayal of rape, murder, the trafficking of women, and lesbianism, Larsson risked voyeuristically reproducing the very misogyny and homophobia he ostensibly seeks to expose and critique.[37] Yet Larsson was mindful of the politics of representation; justice for Lisbeth Salander relies on reframing her sympathetically in the public eye. As a journalist, Mikael Blomkvist makes this point explicit in his e-mail to Salander in the third novel: "Lisbeth—seriously—this battle is going to be decided in the mass media, and not in the courtroom."[38] He asks for her permission to go public with details about her identity and her past, saying, "I have to be able to construct a completely new media image of you, even if that, in your opinion, means invading your privacy—preferably with your approval."[39]

Larsson has tapped into a cultural obsession with sexual deviance, which is cleverly framed as the obsession of the media with, for example, their relentless coverage of Salander as a lesbian psychopath. Blomkvist's stated objective is to portray the unadulterated "truth" about Salander that accounts for her deviance, violence, and involuntary institutionalization. The story offers its reader the possibility of a genderqueer protagonist, while at the same time relegating the exploitation of sexual deviance to the portrayal of police and media corruption. As a genderqueer subject, Salander illustrates key aspects of gender theory, while simultaneously challenging sexual power and gender violence. She is a compelling—if unlikely—feminist figure.

NOTES

1. Stieg Larsson, *The Girl Who Played with Fire*, trans. Reg Keeland (New York: Vintage, 2010), p. 325.

2. The original title of the first novel and film was *Men Who Hate Women*, which was subsequently changed to *The Girl with the Dragon Tattoo* in the English translation.

3. Sara Nelson, the books director of *O: The Oprah Magazine*, points to ambiguity as part of Salander's appeal, stating in an interview that "she's not terribly well defined" (Scott Timberg, "Stieg Larsson's 'Girl' Is an International Publishing Phenomenon," *LA Times*, October 28, 2010).

4. I use this term broadly to refer to a form of transgenderism, including all expressions of gender identity that oppose and resist the conventional binary of masculine male/feminine female.

5. Linda Martin Alcoff, "Cultural Feminism versus Post-Structuralism: The Identity Crisis in Feminist Theory," *Signs* 3 (1988): 406.

6. Julia Serano, *Whipping Girl: A Transsexual Woman on Sexism and the Scapegoating of Femininity* (Berkeley, CA: Seal Press, 2007), p. 330.

7. Ibid., p. 331.

8. Annamarie Jagose, *Queer Theory: An Introduction* (New York: NYU Press, 1996), p. 130.

9. Stieg Larsson, *The Girl with the Dragon Tattoo*, trans. Reg Keeland (New York: Vintage, 2009), p. 38.

10. Ibid., p. 43. In fact, the reverse is also true; when searching for the fugitive Salander in the second novel, police mistake a fourteen-year-old boy for her and attempt to arrest him. Genderqueer people on the FTM spectrum are frequently misperceived as being much younger than their chronological age, a phenomenon rather humorously illustrated in Dorr Legg's encounter with FTM philanthropist Reed Erickson in 1964, whom he described as someone "who looked to me like a blonde high school kid." Erickson was forty-seven at the time. See Aaron H. Devor and Nicholas Matte, "ONE Inc and Reed Erickson: The Uneasy Collaboration of Gay and Trans Activism, 1964–2003," in Stryker and Whittle, eds., *Transgender Studies Reader* (New York: Routledge, 2006), p. 394.

11. Larsson, *The Girl Who Played with Fire*, p. 556.

12. Jenni Miller, "Lisbeth Salander: Not Just Another 'Petite' Powerhouse," *Moviefone
.com*, June 29, 2010, http://blog.moviefone.com/2010/06/29/lisbeth-salander-not-just-
another-petite-powerhouse.

13. Riki Anne Wilchins, "Deconstructing Trans," in Nestle, Wilchins, and Howell,
eds., *GenderQueer: Voices from beyond the Gender Binary* (Boston: Alyson Books, 2002),
pp. 57–58.

14. Judith Butler, *Gender Trouble: Feminism and the Subversion of Identity* (New York:
Routledge, 1990), p. 6.

15. Judith Halberstam, *Female Masculinity* (Durham: Duke University Press, 1998).

16. Arden Niels Oplev, director, and Noomi Rapace, performer, *The Girl with the
Dragon Tattoo (Män som hatar kvinnor)*. Interview with Noomi Rapace, Music Box Films,
2009, DVD.

17. Melissa Silverstein, "Meeting the Girl with the Dragon Tattoo," *Women and Hollywood*,
October 29, 2010, http://womenandhollywood.com/2010/10/29/meeting-the-girl-with-
the-dragon-tattoo/.

18. Michael Kimmel, "Men, Masculinity, and the Rape Culture," in Fletcher, Buchwald,
and Roth, eds. *Transforming a Rape Culture: Revised Edition* (Minneapolis: Milkweed
Editions, 2005), pp. 141–142.

19. Larsson, *The Girl with the Dragon Tattoo*, p. 228.

20. Larsson, *The Girl Who Played with Fire*, p. 129.

21. Butler, *Gender Trouble*.

22. "Gender is the repeated stylization of the body, a set of repeated acts within a highly
rigid regulatory frame that congeal over time to produce the appearance of substance, of
a natural sort of being" (Butler, *Gender Trouble*, p. 33).

23. Larsson, *The Girl Who Played with Fire*, p. 19.

24. Ibid., p. 103.

25. Michel Foucault, *The History of Sexuality: An Introduction, Vol. 1* (New York: Random
House–Vintage, 1990).

26. In the United States, for example, homosexuality was listed as a mental illness in
the *Diagnostic and Statistical Manual of Mental Disorders* (DSM) until 1973, with the
result that many gay men and lesbians were institutionalized prior to that time. Gender
Identity Disorder (GID) continues to be listed in the DSM, pathologizing genderqueer
and transgender people as mentally ill. Cases of institutionalization as a result of this
diagnosis continue to be documented; Daphne Scholinski's autobiography *The Last Time
I Wore a Dress* (New York: Penguin-Riverhead, 1998) is one such example.

27. Foucault, *The History of Sexuality*, pp. 44–45.

28. Larsson, *The Girl with the Dragon Tattoo*, p. 326.

29. Ibid., p. 327.

30. Ibid., p. 396.

31. Larsson, *The Girl Who Played with Fire*, pp. 121–122.

32. Stieg Larsson, *The Girl Who Kicked the Hornet's Nest*, trans. Reg Keeland (New York:
Alfred A. Knopf, 2010), p. 171.

33. This substitution of disability for psychosis is interesting, in that it suggests an explanation for Salander's antisocial and non-normatively gendered behavior. Such a diagnosis can nevertheless be seen as further solidification of Salander as a genderqueer figure, however, in that males are diagnosed with Asperger's four times more frequently than are females.

34. Larsson, *The Girl with the Dragon Tattoo*, p. 200.

35. Ibid., p. 227.

36. Ibid., p. 263.

37. See chapter 10, "The Dragon Tattoo and the Voyeuristic Reader," by Jaime Weida in this book.

38. Larsson, *The Girl Who Kicked the Hornet's Nest*, p. 247.

39. Ibid., p. 248.

PART TWO

MIKAEL "DO-GOODER" BLOMKVIST

If you would be a real seeker after truth, it is necessary that at least once in your life you doubt, as far as possible, all things.

—René Descartes

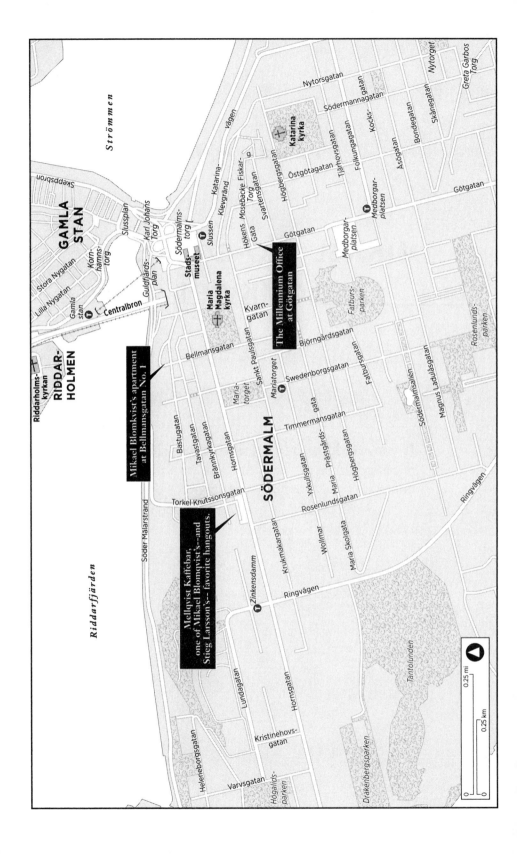

WHY ARE SO MANY WOMEN F***ING KALLE BLOMKVIST?: LARSSON'S PHILOSOPHY OF FEMALE ATTRACTION

Andrew Terjesen and Jenny Terjesen

Mikael Blomkvist gets more play than Journey at a karaoke bar. He's had sexual relationships with Erika Berger, Lisbeth Salander, Cecilia Vanger, Harriet Vanger, and Monica Figuerola, and that's just in the three books we have from Stieg Larsson. Now, if your image of Mikael Blomkvist is Daniel Craig, this might make sense. But if your image of Mikael Blomkvist is Michael Nyqvist (from the Swedish films), it's a little less believable.[1] (Unless you're really into Michael Nyqvist. Sorry.)

In *The Girl Who Played with Fire*, we're told that Blomkvist "knew he was reasonably good-looking, but he had never considered himself exceptionally attractive."[2] That doesn't sound like Daniel Craig. It might even fall short of Michael Nyqvist's understated Swedish smoldering. So how is it that Blomkvist is able to attract such powerful women and bed them without even having to proposition them?

Larsson seems to recognize that there is something unusual about Blomkvist's appeal because he feels it necessary to explain it: "he had often been told that he had something that made women interested in him."[3] Our goal is to try and figure out what that "something" is (and how to bottle it). We don't think it's just his *kevorka* or the steady diet of coffee and sandwiches. Rather, Larsson's female characters are attracted to Blomkvist because he successfully walks the line between respecting women and treating them like shit.

All Out of Love

Millennium editor in chief Erika Berger is Mikael's longest-lasting relationship, but their bond defies the expectations of most male-female relationships. Berger is Blomkvist's best friend. They also sleep together on a regular basis. Her husband knows about all this and has no problem with it. Really, that's fucked up, right? Berger gives us her own explanation of Blomkvist's mysterious appeal. She says, "He radiated self-confidence and security at the same time. . . . He had an ability to make women feel at ease. Going to bed with him was not threatening or complicated, but it might be erotically enjoyable."[4] Blomkvist's sex appeal for Erika boils down to the fact that she can get what she wants from him, and he can't make her do anything she doesn't want to do. (So maybe Berger successfully walks the line between respecting Blomkvist and treating him like shit.)

The philosopher Immanuel Kant (1724–1804) believed that sex was inherently bad for people, no matter who you have it with. According to Kant, sexual attraction "makes of the loved person an Object of appetite; as soon as that appetite has been stilled, the person is cast aside as one casts away a lemon which has been sucked dry. . . . Taken by itself it is a degradation of human nature."[5] This may sound strange to most of us, but Kant's point is that we don't experience desire for a particular man or woman; what we desire is simply sex or a release of tension. We're not thinking about the other person when we're trying to satisfy our own appetites. In satisfying those appetites, we couldn't care less about that person. For Kant, this is morally unacceptable. His moral theory can be summed up in the following maxim: "Act in such a way that you treat humanity, whether in your own person or in the person of another, always at the same time as an end and never simply as a means."[6] By "humanity," Kant meant the part of us that chooses, plans, aspires, and does anything else we associate with free will. To treat humanity as an end would mean to honor the free will of every person.

From Kant's perspective, "sexuality is not an inclination which one human being has for another as such. . . . The desire which a man has for a woman is not directed towards her because she is a human being, but because she is a woman; that she is a human being is of no concern to the man; only her sex is the object of his desires."[7] What Kant was saying is that no one is attracted to someone just because of his or her sparkling personality. Because sexual desire is only about physical gratification, Kant's point is that when we have sex, we allow ourselves to become the instrument for satisfying someone else's desires. Whether we want to admit it or not, we become indistinguishable from a sex toy during the sex act. And no one really worries about the aspirations or the free will of sex toys.

In his relationship with Erika, it certainly seems that Blomkvist is Erika's instrument in satisfying her desires, much more so than she is his.

> During the eighties, when they were not bound by other relationships, they had talked of moving in together. He had wanted to, but Erika always backed out at

the last minute. It wouldn't work, she said, they would risk what they had if they fell in love, too. Blomkvist had often wondered whether it were possible to be more possessed by desire for any other woman. The fact was that they functioned well together, and they had a connection as addictive as heroin.[8]

Clearly, Mikael is interested in forming a more serious relationship with Erika, but she is the one who always pulls back. Erika wants to have her cake and eat it, too. She much prefers their long-standing arrangement, in which she is able to have sex with Mikael on a regular basis but also go home to her husband, Greger Beckman, who strangely accepts that Erika will spend half of her vacation with him and half with Mikael. If Erika could have her way, she would have a threesome with both Greger and Mikael, but Mikael is far too straight for that. This just demonstrates how much her desires seem to disregard Mikael's personhood (and possibly Beckman's, too, although he seems okay with threesomes).

To be fair, Kant was not entirely down on sex. He did admit that sex is not inherently dehumanizing as long as "while one person is acquired by the other as if it were a thing, the one who is acquired acquires the other in turn; for in this way each reclaims itself and restores its personality."[9] In other words, it is not dehumanizing if we both own each other and therefore both still have control of our humanity. For Kant, that happens only in the context of marriage. Yet Berger and Blomkvist's relationship doesn't much resemble anything like mutual ownership of each other. In fact, Berger seems to be the controlling partner in her relationships with both Blomkvist and Beckman, and Blomkvist seems to want absolutely nothing to do with owning anyone else. So while Kant was not entirely down on sex, it is highly unlikely he would have accepted the promiscuous extramarital ways of Kalle Fucking Blomkvist as being anything other than dehumanizing.

Mikael and Erika's relationship also seems to confirm contemporary philosopher Bernard Baumrim's claim that "sexual interaction is essentially manipulative—physically, psychologically, emotionally and even intellectually."[10] The art of attraction is often manipulative and deceitful, in and of itself. People dress themselves up, camouflage flaws, and generally attempt to project a healthy, fit, and financially successful image in order to attract a sexual partner. Baumrim's view of sex seems based on the recognition that deceit and manipulation are part of the game, and the head games that permeate Berger and Blomkvist's long-standing relationship could serve as an excellent argument for such a view.

Although Blomkvist cannot seem to stay away from Berger indefinitely, Berger isn't always available. On their "breaks," Blomkvist isn't the celibate type. In fact, he finds willing sexual partners in the most unlikely of places. The question then might become, is it wrong to use someone if you're up front with the person and say you'd like to use him or her? Blomkvist and Berger have an "understanding." Is that what they understand? If so, at least Blomkvist has a track record of being fairly open about his intentions. During Blomkvist's "break" from Berger, and before Blomkvist sleeps with Salander, he sleeps with Cecilia Vanger. Cecilia, using a phrase she takes directly from Mikael, tells him clearly that she is also just looking for "an occasional lover."[11] Whether she's looking for sex, a pleasant distraction, or information on Blomkvist's investigation into Harriet's disappearance, if that's not saying, "I'd like to use you for a bit," what is? And Blomkvist seems to have no problem with it at all.

Lonely Is the Night

Blomkvist and Salander investigate each other before they even meet. The investigations may have sparked some mutual interest, but it isn't sexual interest at first. Salander is different from any woman Blomkvist has ever met, but he's more intrigued than threatened by her. And Blomkvist is definitely like no man Salander has ever met.

Blomkvist doesn't flirt with Salander. He simply works with her and treats her like a human being. After a few weeks of building professional rapport and a friendly relationship, Salander propositions Blomkvist for sex. What prompts Salander unbidden to come into Blomkvist's room wrapped in a sheet, take his book, and bite his nipple is not exactly clear. What appears to have happened is that Blomkvist, like the investigation she's working on with him, has gotten under her skin. In the time they know each other, Salander opens up more to Blomkvist than she has to any other person in her life. For example, he knows about her being the best hacker in Sweden (and even her closest girlfriend, Mimmi Wu, doesn't know that). With Blomkvist, Salander has achieved something like intimacy. Yet whether it is this budding intimacy or simply sexual frustration that prompts her to get naked with him is unclear to readers and perhaps to Salander herself.

Uncharacteristically, Blomkvist has reservations about having sex with Salander, saying they have to work together, saying he doesn't have a condom. But Salander doesn't see working with Blomkvist after having sex as a problem. She does see rejection and/or sexual frustration as a problem. Blomkvist is the one who is worried about muddying the terms of their relationship. On the surface, it seems that Kant was right: Salander is simply looking to take care of her needs.

The prevailing pop culture wisdom is that relationships based on intense circumstances never last. This seems to hold true for Blomkvist and Salander after their brush with serial killer Martin Vanger. After solving the mystery of Harriet's disappearance (and the murders of a number of women during the last few decades), Salander stays with Blomkvist about five weeks in Sandhamn (where Blomkvist brings only important ladies). While in Sandhamn, their relationship seems to become more than friends with benefits. At least, it does to Salander. Salander begins to think of this time as the first holiday of her life, falling into a routine that revolves around Blomkvist and his work schedule. She's the one who has to drag him up to bed in order to satisfy her needs. Blomkvist is in no hurry to define their relationship, but Salander begins to feel the need to do just that. She is the one who needs to analyze her feelings and the situation.

> Her problem was that she could not interpret her own feelings for him. Not since before reaching puberty had she lowered her guard to let another person get so close as she had with him. . . . It frightened her and made her feel naked and vulnerable to his will.
>
> At the same time—when she looked down at his slumbering form and listened to him snoring—she felt that she had never before in her life had such a trust in another human being.[12]

It is at this point that Salander discovers she's in love with Blomkvist. She reacts to this discovery with reserve, probably because she views the vulnerability that her feelings create as weakness. Whether she intends it or not, her view of the dangers of sexual and romantic relationships is similar to that of Kant and Baumrim. Someone will get used. Someone will get hurt.

It's not that Blomkvist would intentionally harm her. Salander is very certain that it's not in his nature to do that. Yet she's now in uncharted territory with him. She's certainly had sexual relationships with people in the past, and those relationships were about sex, not intimacy. This is her first intimate sexual relationship, and it's Blomkvist's very insistence on always being friends and lovers that has put her in this position.

Yet Salander moves past her fear of being vulnerable and hurt. She cleans her apartment (not routine for her), and then she sits and thinks about what she wants from her relationship with Blomkvist. She wants intimacy: to feel loved and accepted and cherished. She finds an Elvis advertisement for the cabin in Sandhamn as a special Christmas present for Blomkvist and heads out to tell him how she feels. She arrives just in time to see him and Erika Berger pre-shag (ending their "breakup" period). If that ain't a kick in the head. . . .

In Blomkvist's defense, he has no reason to think that Salander was looking for anything more than casual sex. In fact, it's likely that Salander didn't think she was looking for anything else, at least at the start of the relationship.

Even the Nights Are Better

It's easy to understand why women might be attracted to self-confidence and security. A man who is plagued by doubts or the constant need for reassurance can be a real chore. A confident man is someone women can respect and want to partner with, much as Erika has partnered with Mikael on *Millennium*. He's as much a confidant and a friend as he is a sex partner, and what woman doesn't want to have uncomplicated sex with someone she likes? Certainly, most of the men in the world of *The Millennium Trilogy* are patronizing at best and completely misogynistic at worst. In that company, Mikael's certainly not a bad option.

Blomkvist isn't looking for a monogamous sexual relationship, but that doesn't mean that he's not looking for connection with the women he sleeps with. In fact, he insists on a friendly level of intimacy. As we've already seen, the women whom he gets involved with are women he respects as people and as friends. For example, he vouches for Harriet to Erika, telling her, "She deserves respect. And she's a hell of a businesswoman."[13] In light of the way most businessmen treat women in *The Millennium Trilogy*, Mikael's high regard for Harriet's acumen is noteworthy. He even remains friends with his ex-wife Monica Abrahamsson after a divorce that was very painful to both of them. And as his zealous defense of Lisbeth demonstrates, Blomkvist goes to the mattresses for his friends (and, in a staggering number of instances, *with* his friends). His fierce loyalty is something that Erika admires. She's not only attracted to his physical body; she is attracted to his personality and especially the extent to which he treats his friends as ends and not merely as means. Perhaps the reason that Kant was so down on sex was that he couldn't imagine someone who was able to desire a person, sexually and as a friend, and to express that desire in a way that was not manipulative.

Not every philosopher is as down on sex and love as Kant and Baumrim are. Irving Singer is a very sex-positive philosopher who openly disagrees with Kant, pointing out that "Even where a man desires a woman for her sexuality alone, it would be erroneous to think that he cannot be responding to her as a person. For her personality reveals itself in the kind of sexual entity she is for him."[14] Singer argues that Kant is being too simplistic in his view of sexual desire. Sure, we might be drawn to someone's eyes or buttocks, but it is impossible for us to focus entirely on that body part and ignore the person who is blinking or shaking that booty. Unless one is in love with the Cheshire Cat, it's impossible to completely focus only on a single body part. In fact, Singer points out, sexual desire makes us aware of other people as we move beyond body parts to the rest of the body and the mind that moves them. According to Singer, "By awakening us to the living presence of someone else, sexuality can enable us to treat this other being as just the person he or she happens to be."[15] Sex doesn't turn us into objects; it opens us up to people by creating opportunities for greater intimacy.

In each of his relationships, Blomkvist seems to navigate very intricate professional and personal boundaries. With Erika, things seem to wax and wane, depending on how involved they both are in *Millennium*. His relationships with Cecilia and

Harriet arise out of investigations and his work at *Millennium*. There are, then, a couple of catalysts for his sexual encounters, the first being the professional respect he clearly demonstrates and the second being sexual intimacy with no games or deception. Going to bed with Blomkvist is straightforward; there are no strings, no attempts to control the women he sleeps with. He works alongside them as equals, and he absolutely respects their choices, both professionally and personally.

In fact, many of these women are his social betters. Erika, Cecilia, and Harriet are all from upper-class families, while Mikael's background is working class. Undoubtedly, they are attracted to Mikael in part because he does not feel threatened by a richer woman. In the case of Cecilia and Harriet, he is also not concerned that each is about a decade or so older than he is. Blomkvist's ability to see past age and class are evidence that he is interested in these women as individuals and not merely as sexual partners who fit some socially prescribed ideal of desirability or attraction.

When Lisbeth meets Blomkvist for the first time, he shows up at her apartment unannounced, which freaks her out. The fact that they already know so much about each other limits Blomkvist's and Salander's ability to deceive the other in the ways we often attempt to project ourselves on meeting someone new, and it leaves room for mutual respect for each other's skills.

Salander comes to the door wrapped in a sheet, and he invites himself in, starts cleaning up her kitchen, and offers her bagels. When he tells her he knows she's a computer hacker, he manages to do so in a manner that is not completely threatening to Lisbeth, acknowledging that Lisbeth also knows most of his secrets, as well. Blomkvist says, "I can't compete with you. I've only done a rapid routine check. . . . But you certainly know a great deal about me. Much of which is private, dammit, things that only my closest friends know."[16] Blomkvist's cards-on-the-table approach acknowledges both that Salander is his equal in investigating and that she already knows as much about him as his friends do. "And now here I am sitting in your kitchen and eating bagels with you. We have known each other half an hour, but I have the feeling that we've been friends for years. Does that make sense to you?"[17]

As they begin working together, Salander is impressed by how different Blomkvist seems to be from other men. On the one hand, "Blomkvist had the same tiresome habits as everyone else, poking around in her life and asking questions," but on the other hand, when Lisbeth is her usual close-lipped self, he behaves in an unusual manner: "When she ignored his questions he simply shrugged and left her in peace. Astounding."[18] Salander expects confrontation with Blomkvist when her first move on the case is to transfer all of the info on his iBook to her own computer. Blomkvist just gives her a resigned look and a sarcastic mutter before showering and then discussing the case with her. He has enough confidence to trust her.

The One That You Love

Monica Figuerola is a powerful woman, physically, intellectually, and professionally. An attractive woman as well, she is accustomed to men around her acting out of insecurity or feeling threatened by her, both professionally and personally. Blomkvist is fascinated by her well-defined physique, and when she says to him, "Maybe you're just bothered by seeing a woman with muscles. Do you think it's a turn-off, or unfeminine?" he quickly responds, "No, not at all. It suits you somehow. You're very sexy."[19]

The idea that men find her threatening is very much on Monica's mind (and perhaps on the minds of many of the powerful women whom Blomkvist becomes involved with). After they sleep together the first time, Monica explains that she hasn't had many relationships because, as she says, "I've noticed that quite a few men get interested, but then they start challenging me and looking for ways to dominate me. Especially if they discover I'm a policewoman." Mikael dismisses her concern, telling her, "I'm not going to compete with you. I'm better than you are at what I do. And you're better than I am at what you do."[20] In their exchange, we again see Mikael's respect for the talents and skills of the women he sleeps with and how his own confidence in himself is not shaken.

Unlike his other sexual partners, Monica will not accept an undefined understanding between them, and it's clear that undefined understandings are Mikael's preferred MO. When Monica asks him point-blank whether he loves Berger or Salander, his response is noncommittal: "If love is liking someone an awful lot, then I suppose I'm in love with several people."[21] Monica is not terribly pleased with his answer:

> "But it does bother me that I don't really know what's happening between us. And I don't think I can have a relationship with a man who screws around whenever he feels like it."
>
> "I'm not going to apologize for the way I've led my life."
>
> "And I guess that in some way I'm falling for you because you are who you are. It's easy to sleep with you because there's no bullshit and you make me feel safe. But this all started because I gave in to a crazy impulse. It doesn't happen very often, and I hadn't planned it. And now we've gotten to the stage where I've become just another one of the girls you invite out here."
>
> They sat in silence for a moment.
>
> "You didn't have to come."[22]

Monica wins major points for not punching Blomkvist at that moment.

As with the other women in Blomkvist's life, the draw for Monica is the way Mikael treats her: like an adult, like an equal, and in a way that would make Kant proud (except for the sex).[23] Yet Monica expresses a lot of concern for how things might inevitably go. Even when Mikael voices regret over the breakup of his marriage, which he admits fell apart because he could not stay away from Erika, the greatest commitment he can offer to Monica is that he's terrified of losing her. And she "suddenly felt a great sadness."[24] Doesn't exactly bode well for Monica.

There is hope for the relationship when Erika agrees to back off after a weak rejection from Mikael, in which he tells her, "I think I'm in love with [Monica], too." Yet just how far Erika is backing off is still to be determined: "'I promise I'll keep my distance until, you know . . . well, maybe,' she said."[25] Erika's "promise" indicates that she basically assumes the whole Figuerola relationship will fall apart sooner or later, and then Erika will be there, and her arrangement with Mikael can continue just as it has before. Perhaps Salander should have gone through with her impulse and used the Elvis sign to cleave Erika's head when she had the opportunity.

Just as I Am

If anyone has Blomkvist pegged, it's his sister Annika. Guessing that Mikael has done it again, she tells Lisbeth, "My brother is completely irresponsible when it comes to relationships. He screws his way through life and doesn't seem to grasp how much it can hurt those women who think of him as more than a casual affair."[26] Annika's analysis makes Blomkvist sound like almost every other man in *The Millennium Trilogy*, but he's not. His behavior may be similar and may produce the same effects, but it is motivated by a very different attitude than that of the men who hate women. What attracts women to him, as we've seen, is that he never objectifies them or tries to control them. He sees them as no different than himself. Unfortunately, he lacks interest in any longer-term commitment. Perhaps he actually accepts Kant's and Baumrim's assertion that sexual love inevitably turns partners into objects.

Although he is pretty bad at sustaining sexual relationships, other than the Berger exception, he is very good at forming friendships. Mikael makes it very clear that he sees all of these women as friends. At the end of *The Girl Who Kicked the Hornet's Nest*, Lisbeth finally comes to realize that Blomkvist is actually a much better friend than he is a lover. In a parallel to their first meeting, Blomkvist shows up unannounced with bagels. Salander greets him, wrapped in a towel.

> In real life, standing on her doorstep, he was still fucking attractive. And he knew her secrets, just as she knew all of his.
>
> She looked at him for a moment and realized that she now had no feelings for him. At least not those kind of feelings.
>
> He had in fact been a good friend to her over the past year.[27]

In light of the fact that his relationships are founded on a friendship of equals, we should probably cut Blomkvist a little slack when it comes to his failed romantic relationships. The problem for Blomkvist seems to be an unwillingness to define his relationships, as if the process of defining leads to power struggles and control issues. When thinking about his relationship with Lisbeth, he is reluctant even to refer to himself as her "ex-boyfriend."[28] Blomkvist breaks his own rules in continually returning to Lisbeth's apartment, even when he fears it shows a lack of respect for her, which is not the case. He seeks her out as a concerned friend and because he misses her, but not because he wants to be with her. It's difficult for most of us to delineate the distinctions between friend and lover. When forced to, most of us will move to the friend zone because it is easier to understand and to determine the correct way to treat one another as friends.

When Salander is gravely wounded at the end of *The Girl Who Played with Fire*, her last conscious thoughts are of Mimmi, not of Mikael. Perhaps unconsciously, Lisbeth understands that although she cannot completely define what her relationship to Mimmi is, Mimmi is hers. Mimmi, in some sense, belongs to Salander, and she can't really say that about Mikael. It's difficult to say whether Blomkvist doesn't want to "be owned" by anyone or whether he just doesn't want to "own" anyone else. Either way, he avoids any relationship that could lead to one or the other.

What Salander and Monica Figuerola want from Mikael is very specific: it is to feel loved, accepted, and cherished. It is the "cherished" part that Blomkvist has trouble with.[29] To cherish a lover is to distinguish him or her above all others, to define each other exclusively.[30] When we cherish, we possess each other, and we give and take power. Perhaps as someone who has dedicated his professional life to exposing the corruption that inevitably comes from unchecked power, Mikael believes one cannot avoid corruption or prevent abuses of power in a relationship on those terms. Lisbeth may realize that Mikael would rather avoid the difficulties of defining each other (maybe out of fear that it's impossible to do so and to remain friends and equals). Ultimately, it's a bit of cowardice on Mikael's part, because, as Singer argues, it is possible to balance friendship, sex, and love. Thankfully for the women, it's not that "he's just not that into you." It's that "he totally respects you too much to objectify you by making you his girlfriend." Because that line works, right?

NOTES

1. And if your image of Blomkvist is Stieg Larsson, it makes no sense whatsoever.

2. Stieg Larsson, *The Girl Who Played with Fire*, trans. Reg Keeland (New York: Vintage, 2010), p. 42.

3. Ibid.

4. Ibid.

5. Immanuel Kant, *Lectures on Ethics*, trans. Louis Infield (Indianapolis: Hackett, 1963), p. 163.

6. Immanuel Kant, *Grounding for the Metaphysics of Morals*, trans. James W. Ellington (Indianapolis: Hackett, 1993), p. 36. See chapter 15 in this book, "Acting Out of Duty or Just Acting Out? Salander and Kant," by Tanja Barazon.

7. Kant, *Lectures on Ethics*, p. 164.

8. Stieg Larsson, *The Girl with the Dragon Tattoo*, trans. Reg Keeland (New York: Vintage, 2009), p. 62.

9. Immanuel Kant, *The Metaphysics of Morals*, trans. Mary Gregor (Cambridge: Cambridge University Press, 1991), p. 97.

10. Bernard Baumrim, "Sexual Immorality Delineated," in Robert Baker and Frederick Elliston, eds., *Philosophy and Sex*, 2nd ed. (Buffalo, NY: Prometheus, 1984), p. 300.

11. Larsson, *The Girl with the Dragon Tattoo*, p. 21.

12. Ibid., p. 583.

13. Ibid., p. 544.

14. Irving Singer, *The Nature of Love, Vol. 2: Courtly and Romantic Love* (Chicago: University of Chicago Press, 1984), p. 382.

15. Ibid.

16. Larsson, *The Girl with the Dragon Tattoo*, p. 332.

17. Ibid.

18. Ibid., p. 394.

19. Stieg Larsson, *The Girl Who Kicked the Hornet's Nest*, trans. Reg Keeland (New York: Alfred A. Knopf, 2010), p. 322.

20. Ibid., p. 344.

21. Ibid., p. 423.

22. Ibid.

23. Singer actually argues that Kant's discussion of marriage is really applicable to all sexual relationships, as long as both partners are open to each other.

24. Larsson, *The Girl Who Kicked the Hornet's Nest*, p. 424.

25. Ibid., p. 517.

26. Ibid., p. 519.

27. Ibid., pp. 562–563.

28. Larsson, *The Girl Who Played with Fire*, p. 17.

29. Maybe Kant was right to limit his caveat to marriage, in which we promise to love, honor, and obey, because without such an explicit promise, someone like Blomkvist can cease to treat people as special in the way all of us want to be treated. Blomkvist respects all women, but he is not so good at respecting them as individuals.

30. Whether exclusivity is a requirement for romantic relationships is something that philosophers have argued over. Mikael seems to think it's not, or that if it is, exclusivity could be defined as "ladies who have been to Sandhamn." We would argue that Mikael's own sexual history reveals the problems in not committing exclusively to a beloved (single, one at a time).

WHY JOURNALISTS AND GENIUSES LOVE COFFEE AND HATE THEMSELVES

Eric Bronson

Mikael Blomkvist is "like some fucking macho cowboy," who can "vacillate between self-absorption and depression."[1] He is also morally "naïve" and "quite predictable."[2] And that's just what the women who love him have to say. We, too, might tolerate his eccentricities and forgive him for his character flaws if we could only understand one thing. Thermos after thermos, Blomkvist tries our patience and leaves us always with the same burning question: *What's the deal with all that coffee?*

In fact, nearly all of Stieg Larsson's characters drink coffee: in the morning, at work, among friends at a café, before sex (Lisbeth and Mimmi Wu can't wait and let their coffee get cold), before committing murder (Gullberg), before getting murdered (Björck), after stumbling onto a murder scene (Blomkvist), and the list goes on. Seriously, do they really need that much caffeine? Coffee doesn't even taste all that good. As behavioral psychologist Robert Bolles wrote, "Children do not like it, uninitiated adults do not like it, rats do not like it: nobody likes coffee except those who have drunk a fair amount of it, and they all love it."[3] To put it even more plainly, on a Stieg Larsson fan website, girl_interrupted from Australia wrote,

> theyr really addicted. . . . shud seek help . . .
>   i cant imagine it can be healthy to drink so much coffee in one day . . .
>   it made me wanna drink coffee!!!!![4]

Why do we get so much pleasure out of drinking something we don't entirely like? This difficult philosophical question takes us back to Europe's first coffeehouses. There we find that coffee and philosophy go together like Swedish meatballs and a tall glass of kefir.

A Krona for Your Thoughts

When European philosophers took their first swigs of coffee in the seventeenth century, they did what such profound thinkers typically do. They got carried away. It wasn't long before the concept of hanging out with genteel company and idling away hours at a time attracted deadbeat husbands everywhere. In one anonymous story from seventeenth-century England, two "Maidens" voice their disgust with this black "liquor" sold alongside hot chocolate at places of dubious repute. "I believe the Devil first invented this liquor, on purpose to plague our Sex," says one distraught woman. "I imagine so too," her friend responds, "but rather then I'll dote upon a man that drinks *Coffee*, I am resolv'd to lead Apes in Hell."[5]

Philosophers who preferred *not* to lead apes in hell congregated in coffeehouses to discuss the serious issues of the day. The establishments became known as "penny universities" because one small coin bought a thoughtful man a lot more than coffee. Listening to the discussion and the debates was an education, one that was otherwise closed to many a poor student who could not possibly enter a real university. In 1711, Joseph Addison claimed that by collecting bits of wisdom from coffeehouses, his newspaper, *The Spectator*, was following a long-standing philosophical tradition. "It was said of Socrates that he brought Philosophy down from the Heaven, to inhabit among men, and I shall be ambitious to have it said of me, that I have brought Philosophy out of Closets and Libraries, Schools and Colleges, to dwell in . . . Coffee-Houses."[6]

Order and logic ruled the coffeehouse in the early 1700s. The intellectual conversation was stimulating and inspiring, like a Bach cantata. Not surprisingly, in Leipzig the maestro led his own coffeehouse band at Zimmerman's Café. Bach's soulful ditties were always well-received, especially when his singer launched into the rousing "Coffee Cantata."

> If I can't drink
> my bowl of coffee three times daily,
> then in my torment I will shrivel up
> like a piece of roast goat.[7]

It's unclear whether European philosophers who frequented cafés such as Zimmerman's really did believe that their coffee tasted "more delicious than a thousand kisses," as Bach's singer proclaimed, but more and more frequently, philosophers turned toward the fraternity of like-minded men, swapping Enlightenment theories and swilling oily bliss. "In my case my thoughts are my wenches," wrote French philosopher Denis Diderot (1713–1784), before heading off to the Café de la Régence.[8] As cofounder and chief editor of the first modern-day encyclopedia, Diderot knew that some of the best lessons in ethics were taught around the chess tables in the coffeehouses of Paris, "for if you can be a man of wit and a great chess-player . . . you can also be a great chess-player and an ass."[9]

In *The Girl with the Dragon Tattoo*, Henrik Vanger is the embodiment of old-fashioned Enlightenment ethics. He cares about developing his character and fulfilling his duties to society. Coffee, to such a man, is meant to be sipped, not downed. Lofty conversation is prized above all. Vanger is pleased that his "name is a byword for a man who keeps his word and remembers his promises," and he therefore takes his coffee black, "plainly boiled in a pan in true Norrland style."[10]

Blomkvist, the consummate multitasker, quickly grows impatient and puts Vanger on the clock. Yet by the end of the first book, when Blomkvist is back in the countryside, hunting for photos of Children's Day, he finally learns his lesson. It's time to put the watch away once the coffee is brewed. Even today, there remain places where coffee goes hand in hand with community and relationship building, and although Blomkvist "had drunk more coffee during the past twenty-four hours than at any time in his life . . . he had learned that in Norrland it was rude to say no."[11]

Let Them Eat Cake! (but First, a Cup of Coffee)

By the end of the eighteenth century, coffeehouses were becoming hotbeds for philosophical debates on freedom, democracy, and equality. Though the American colonists were more than willing to dump English tea into the Boston harbor, they were understandably reluctant to part with their coffee. The Sons of Liberty protested King George's Stamp Act by staging a funeral for Liberty outside the Merchant's Coffee-House in Philadelphia and burned stamped tax paper inside the coffeehouse in 1776.[12]

Philosophers Karl Marx (1818–1883) and Friedrich Engels (1820–1895) spent many hours at the Café de la Régence in Paris, working out their famous *Communist Manifesto*. Their collaboration ignited interest in coffeehouses across Europe. In Vienna, at the Café Landtmann, philosophers Max Weber (1864–1920) and Josef Schumpeter (1883–1950) met to discuss and debate Marx's communist revolution, which was sweeping through Europe. Before a fistfight erupted, Weber took the high road and stormed out. Schumpeter was unimpressed. Serious plotting should be kept under wraps. "How can a man shout like that in a coffeehouse?" he wondered aloud.[13]

Comrade Lev Trotsky (1879–1940) covertly prepared for *his* role in the revolution by playing chess and sipping coffee in Vienna. When the Austrian foreign minister first heard that the revolution was under way, he was skeptical. "Russia is not a land where revolutions break out," he confidently asserted. "Besides, who on earth would make a revolution in Russia? Perhaps Herr Trotsky from the Café Central?"[14]

Devious plans call for more devious meetings in crowded places, usually over coffee. When creepy Nils Bjurman enlists the even creepier Ronald Niederman to kill Salander, they hatch their diabolical plan at Café Hedon. When Niederman outsources the job to a still creepier biker dude (Lundin) with an "untrustworthy face" and "a mousy moustache," they whisper evil nothings in Blomberg's Café.

Is it ethical to kill someone if the murder will bring happiness to many others? It's an intriguing philosophical question that Fyodor Dostoyevsky (1821–1881) poses in *Crime and Punishment*. Before attempting to kill her father and her half brother, Salander sits in a Göteborg café, sipping a latté while thumbing through Dostoyevsky's masterpiece. Blomkvist might agree with his colleague Malin Eriksson that there are pleasant times when a vodka and lime juice is "much better than another cup of coffee," but if it's death and destruction that you're after, then the right café is crucial.[15]

Take Niederman, for example. Yes, he snaps the necks of innocent victims with his bare hands, but he also loves people. That is, he needs people. When he's alone, Niederman sees forest trolls, leprechauns, and haunting creatures from the underworld that look like enormous stingrays. But when he's surrounded by people he despises, he feels more at ease in the world. Niederman is not the only one. Twentieth-century philosophers and artists didn't think that choosing to be alone among strangers was so unusual. Indeed, anxiety and isolation were common themes in existential philosophies, and as usual, the coffeehouse was the place to make sense of it all.

The Lost Café

After Trotksy left for Russia, the Café Central became a haunt for lost existentialists. As drama critic Alfred Polgar wrote in 1926,

> The Café Central lies on the Viennese latitude at the meridian of loneliness. Its inhabitants are, for the most part, people whose hatred of their fellow human beings is as fierce as their longing for people, who want to be alone but need companionship for it.[16]

Cafés everywhere were becoming "meridians of loneliness." No longer places of revolutions, coffeehouses became associated with the "lost generation," killing time. First coined by the novelist Gertrude Stein (1874–1946) and made popular by Ernest Hemingway (1899–1961), the "lost generation" referred to people who lived through World War I, no longer believing in the sacred cows of the Old World. Abandoned by God, bereft of brotherly love, coffee drinkers turned introspective and solitary. Describing his life in Paris in the 1920s, Hemingway begins his memoirs with a chapter titled "A Good Café on the Place St.-Michel," a lonely outpost where "All of the sadness of the city came suddenly with the first cold rains of winter."[17]

Salander wears her loneliness on her sleeve. Literally. The words I AM AN ALIEN are splayed across her T-shirt, next to a picture of E.T. with fangs. Salander hangs out in coffee shops for the same reason she spends so much time online: "She was simply not very good at establishing contact with other people."[18] Salander and Niederman aren't the only lost souls hanging out in the cafés of Stockholm, though. Instead of surrounding himself with loving friends and family, Blomkvist hears of his ninety-day prison sentence on the radio among strangers, downing (what else?) a latté at the Kafé Anna.

In 1993, American sociologist George Ritzer caused a bit of a stir by claiming that Max Weber was right. Not because he stormed out of a coffee shop, but because he argued that bureaucratic institutions were beginning to dominate our everyday lives. The problem was that these well-organized, rational systems were deeply irrational. In his book *The McDonaldization of Society*, Ritzer claimed that McDonald's has become the poster child for the coldly rational, irrational new world order. That's bad news for Blomkvist, Salander, and the spry ex-boxer Paolo Roberto who really love their burgers. Yet in 2011, Ritzer added a new section—Starbuckization. "Starbucks," Ritzer said, "has most, if not all, of the irrationalities associated with McDonald's (homogenization, disenchantment, dehumanization), as well as additional ones."[19]

Coffeehouses, it would seem, are losing their unique character, and it isn't only the large chains. Take, for example, the cafés on the Boulevard Saint-Germain in Paris where the existentialist philosophers Jean-Paul Sartre (1905–1980) and Simone de Beauvoir (1908–1986) wrote some of their most famous books. At Les Deux Magots, de Beauvoir first conceived of writing *The Second Sex*, still one of the most important books on existential ethics and feminist philosophy. Nowadays, tourists can sit by her plaque and recall her earlier warning to the sub-man: "He discovers around him only an insignificant and dull world. How could this naked world arouse within him any desire to feel, to understand, to live?"[20] A cup of coffee runs more than five bucks at Les Deux Magots, but if you go on Sunday, you can sometimes hear a parrot singing "La Vie en Rose."[21]

These kinds of impersonal gimmicks disgust Salander and Blomkvist, but neither is a stranger to Ritzer's homogenization and disenchantment. Though Larsson makes it quite clear that "crappy pink drinks with stupid umbrellas were not

Salander's style," she has no qualms about regularly eating frozen Billy's Pan Pizza from a nearby 7-Eleven.[22] And when Mia Johansson serves coffee in uniquely fancy porcelain cups passed down from her grandmother, Blomkvist boorishly dismisses the gesture. He "didn't give a damn about flowered coffee cups and instead cast an appraising eye on the plate with the cheesecake."[23]

One for the Road

Lonely, self-absorbed, and socially awkward, today's coffee drinker is again a sign of the times. That's not to say everyone is like that. In most societies, you can still find well-adjusted, contented, and calm people completely at peace with themselves and their universe. Those are the tea drinkers. We like them, generally. They make for good brain surgeons, as Lisbeth learns after getting shot in the head. And when the innocent Caribbean boy seduces her with a cup of tea, we can understand the allure (even though his name is Bland).

Drinking tea is associated with calmness and inner peace. Zen masters drink tea. Buddhist philosopher Daisetz Suzuki (1870–1966) wrote that "the principle of tranquility is something that emanates from one's inner consciousness as it is especially understood in the art of tea." The tea drinker is "able to breathe a spirit of tranquility into all the surrounding objects."[24] If we only took to drinking tea instead of coffee, perhaps the utopias dreamed of by Enlightenment philosophers would already be upon us. "Why not consecrate ourselves to the queen of the Camelias," asks Okakura Kakuzo (1862–1913), "and revel in the warm stream of sympathy that flows from her altar?"[25] In his *Book of Tea*, Kakuzo longs for a time when we put aside our differences and come together to drink from "the cup of humanity."

> Meanwhile, let us have a sip of tea. The afternoon glow is brightening the bamboos, the fountains are bubbling

with delight, the soughing of the pines is heard in our kettle. Let us dream of evanescence, and linger in the beautiful foolishness of things.[26]

Somewhere along the line, Stieg Larsson missed the memo about the dream of evanescence and the queen of the Camelias. Tea just doesn't figure prominently in his story. His characters prefer a quick cup of joe in between kickboxing classes and hacking government websites. Blomkvist once drank so much coffee that it left him "sober and feeling unwell."[27] Perhaps he is not so alone after all.

NOTES

1. Stieg Larsson, *The Girl Who Played with Fire*, trans. Reg Keeland (New York: Vintage, 2010), p. 430.

2. Ibid., pp. 403–404.

3. Brian Cowan, *The Social Life of Coffee: The Emergence of the British Coffeehouse* (New Haven, CT: Yale University Press, 2005), p. 6.

4. See www.stieglarsson.com/discussion-boards/coffee-and-sandwiches-7711611.

5. Anon, "The Maidens complain[t] against coffee, or, The coffee-house discovered beseiged, stormed, taken, untyled and lai[d] open to publick view," electronic reproduction (Ann Arbor, MI: Early English Books, 1641–1700).

6. Markman Ellis, *The Coffee House: A Cultural History* (London: Orion, 2004), p. 185.

7. See www.afactor.net/kitchen/coffee/kaffeeKantate.html.

8. Denis Diderot, *Rameau's Nephew*, in *Rameau's Nephew and D'Alembert's Dream*, trans. Leonard Tancock (Toronto: Penguin, 1966), p. 33.

9. Ibid., p. 33.

10. Stieg Larsson, *The Girl with the Dragon Tattoo*, trans. Reg Keeland (New York: Vintage, 2009), pp. 87, 82.

11. Ibid., p. 365.

12. Ellis, *The Coffee House*, p. 202.

13. Karl Jaspers, "Max Weber as Politician, Scientist, Philosopher," in *Three Essays: Leonardo, Descartes, Max Weber* (New York: Harcourt, 1953), p. 225.

14. Bennett Alan Weinberg and Bonnie K. Bealer, *The World of Caffeine: The Science and Culture of the World's Most Popular Drug* (New York: Routledge, 2001), p. 78.

15. Larsson, *The Girl Who Played with Fire*, p. 301.

16. See depts.washington.edu/vienna/documents/Polgar/Polgar_Cafe.htm.

17. Ernest Hemingway, *A Moveable Feast* (New York: Simon & Schuster, 1964), p. 16.

18. Larsson, *The Girl with the Dragon Tattoo*, p. 235.

19. George Ritzer, *The McDonaldization of Society*, 6th ed. (Thousand Oaks, CA: Pine Forge Press, 2011), p. 224.

20. Simone de Beauvoir, *The Ethics of Ambiguity*, trans. Bernard Frechtman (New York: Citadel, 1948), p. 43.

21. Marie France-Boyer and Eric Morin, *The French Café* (London: Thames and Hudson, 1994), p. 66.

22. Larsson, *The Girl Who Played with Fire*, p. 28.

23. Ibid., p. 96.

24. Daisetz T. Suzuki, *Zen and Japanese Culture* (Princeton, NJ: Princeton University, 1970), p. 306.

25. Okakura Kakuzo, *The Book of Tea* (Rutland, VT: Charles E. Tuttle, 1956), p. 6.

26. Ibid., p. 17.

27. Larsson, *The Girl Who Played with Fire*, p. 221.

THE MAKING
OF KALLE BLOMKVIST:
CRIME JOURNALISM IN
POSTWAR SWEDEN

Ester Pollack

They can be identified from afar: the crime tourists, who with great zeal are searching for locales they have read about, sinking back into the chairs of familiar cafés, climbing the hills of Södermalm, reliving Blomkvist's and Salander's adventures. In my neighborhood, on the island of Södermalm in Stockholm, I keep bumping into fans of Mikael Blomkvist and Lisbeth Salander. They move in groups, looking up at an apartment building on Mosebacke, nodding to one another. "That's where she lived. What a breathtaking view!" Here, on the heights of Södermalm, they gaze out over the inlet to Stockholm, where the Baltic Sea meets Lake Mälaren. Lisbeth's magnificent apartment, purchased with money she cleverly (and probably justifiably, in the reader's eyes) appropriated from the empire of the financial villain Wennerström, is on the top floor of a building on Fiskargatan. The literary tourists sigh: Lisbeth must have had a magnificent panorama over the city and its countless islands.

And so the tour proceeds, to *Millennium*'s editorial office on Götgatsbacken just below Mosebacke, to Blomkvist's loft apartment a few blocks away on Bellmansgatan, and on to the various cafés where crucial meetings and conversations take place in the fictional world of the trilogy. "Excuse me, but where is Salander's first apartment?" inquires a chic Italian woman, clutching one of the novels and a map of Stockholm. It's a late afternoon in August, and she seems to have lost her group, or else she is one of those trying to find her way on her own. We locals point, explain, show the way. City tours following in the footsteps of crime fiction appear to have become part of the Swedish tourism industry. In the small southern town of Ystad, where Henning Mankell's books about Inspector Wallander take place, guided tours have generated a healthy tourist income for years. We who live in Stockholm see the same thing happening in the wake of the success of Stieg Larsson's *Millennium Trilogy*.

Previous chapters in this book have discussed the intense interest in Salander, but what about Blomkvist, the embodiment of the investigative journalist who exposes power and corruption? He's an honest, hardworking watchdog with high ideals, extraordinary intuition, and a nose for what lies hidden beneath the surface: "He had devoted the whole of his professional life to exposing things that other people tried to hide, and his ethics prevented him from taking part in a cover-up of the terrible crimes committed in Martin Vanger's basement. He was doing his duty: revealing the truth."[1] Blomkvist is obstinacy personified, following wherever the scent leads him, often in the face of powerful opposition. He challenges society's institutions, including his own (more cowardly) colleagues in the media.

Does he exist in reality? Certainly—at least, as an ideal that was epitomized by the American journalists Bob Woodward and Carl Bernstein, who exposed the Watergate scandal in the 1970s.

Watergate has become the prime symbol of investigative journalism, underlining the importance of providing the public with an insight into dirty politics—journalism as a counterweight to political power.

Blomkvist represents this counterweight. He is the ultimate muckraker, exposing the economic, political, and juridical elites—as well as clarifying the connections between them. He defends the democratic order but also the ordinary citizen threatened by the corrupt forces of wealth, status, and power. Larsson's journalist hero is capable of drawing aside the veil, revealing the criminal perpetrators, the men who abuse women—and democracy. If we are to truly appreciate Kalle Blomkvist, we need to look at how the real-life character type emerged in Sweden.

The Journalist as a Mouthpiece for Political Power

In the 1950s, concern about juvenile crime was particularly strong in Swedish politics and journalism. The big questions were: Why do people commit crime? And why do youngsters "turn bad"? In the press, much attention was paid to thefts carried out by young boys and their membership in "gangs."[2] Mainstream media outlets decried the lack of institutions adapted to youth issues. It was argued that correctional treatment procedures for young offenders needed reform. The 1950s were fairly tough and traditional in terms of law enforcement, but nonetheless it was the decade with the steepest rise in crime rates.[3]

In journalism, criminal offenders were described as the black sheep of the welfare state, a social category with problems. The "bad guys" could, however, be rehabilitated, and in particular, it was conceivable that young criminals could be returned to the fold. Knowledge, strong institutions, and the correct treatment regimes were all that was needed.

In the welfare state of the 1950s, *the police* were the true heroes in crime journalism. They could run faster than any train to catch a crook, and they were on the scene just in time to defuse any desperado's homemade bomb. Insurance frauds were exposed on a regular basis, youngsters on the skids were put back on track, and forensic specialists had no problem cracking cases involving devious felons. The picture presented to contemporary audiences was that of alert, heroic, and successful crime fighters, who sometimes put their lives on the line to uphold law and order.

In daily life, journalists entered into a kind of symbiotic relationship with the police. Newspapers and radio were direct channels to the public. Through them, it was possible to publish wanted bulletins and, hopefully, enlist the help of observant citizens. The journalist's role was that of public servant, cooperating with the police and the authorities in order to reduce crime and raise awareness of the great welfare edifice being built. Journalists had social responsibility. They were an important mouthpiece for the authorities.

The Journalist as a Critic of the Welfare State

By the 1970s, these same institutions were now being criticized for not meeting the requirements demanded of them. In media debates, the criminal justice and prison system was depicted as being conservative and extremely difficult to reform. The big question of the 1970s was how to humanize the system and fundamentally change the class structure, which was regarded as the root cause of criminal behavior.

In the mid-1970s, Sweden's minister for justice Lennart Geijer radically declared that prisons should be demolished. Prisons had only one purpose: they protected citizens from a small number of violent individuals. Incarceration, Geijer argued, was nothing more than an act of revenge, creating hatred in the people who were forced to endure it, without reducing crime. The justice minister's statements were fully in line with the new conception of crime, which a liberal-radical political movement had been expressing throughout the decade.[4] This movement was manifested in the National Association for the Humanization of the Correctional System (NACS), one of several stakeholders behind the *Pocket Magazine R*. Published in a neat little pocketbook format, the magazine became a driving force in the criminal justice policy debate in the 1970s. It gave voice to a sociopolitical commitment and sided with the weakest members of society, including convicts, substance abusers, alcoholics, and the mentally ill.

Journalists in the 1970s became social critics, pointing out the shortcomings of the authorities.[5] Their professionalism and independence had increased significantly. During this period, the ideal of the investigative and truth-seeking journalist was established. Jan Guillou, a well-known Swedish forerunner to Mikael Blomkvist, had already written a number of high-profile articles when, in 1973, he exposed a secret undercover organization that, among other things, was involved in the systematic monitoring of left-wing supporters.[6] As with the fictional Blomkvist, Guillou was sentenced to a short prison sentence, before taking his revenge on his detractors by proving that he was right.

Guillou also resembles Stieg Larsson. While in prison, Guillou read Sjövall and Wahlöö, the Swedish duo who wrote socially critical crime novels in the 1970s.[7] Guillou in turn wrote a spy thriller for his generation, giving birth to the novels about intelligence officer Carl Hamilton.[8] Guillou's books were extremely successful and were made into movies many times over.[9]

The Journalist as an Interpreter of the Culture of Violence

Two decades later, in the mid-1990s, the picture changed once again, as the balance of power between journalism and politics shifted. Journalism evolved into a social institution, intervening in the workings of institutions and organizations, as well as in the everyday lives of individuals. Journalists who described, debated, and reported crimes were acting out a variety of roles: court reporter, editorial writer, cultural journalist, television host, moderator, panel member, and expert. Crime had become a theme, echoing through numerous media channels as news, information, and entertainment.

Crime journalism in the 1990s focused on the influence of violence, the threat of racism, and the suffering of the victims. Significantly, the victim had increasingly replaced the criminal as the central character. In schools, bullying had become an issue; in health care, staff members were being openly exposed to violence; in the world of sports, hooliganism, spectator violence, and assault were highlighted. There were also reports on neo-Nazi violence, men's violence against women, and sexual abuse of women and children. The picture that emerged was of a violent society with popular racist ideologies.

The youths were described as following a lifestyle of violent crime, whether they were junkies, motorcycle gangsters, racists, football hooligans, thugs, skinheads, or immigrants. Optimism about the future was nonexistent, and rehabilitation ideologies were replaced by calls for tougher sentencing. The situation in the cities was described using war imagery. Young men were "ticking time bombs," and a succession of "gang wars" was threatening the community. Human evil and individual choice were the reasons behind trends in criminality. Ethnicity was also used as an explanation. In journalistic descriptions, youth offenders lacked role models, motivation, and future prospects. Citizens were afraid of falling victim to crime and did not trust the police. All in all, a profoundly pessimistic picture was being painted in the media.

Meanwhile, statistics show that registered youth crimes had, in fact, not increased during that time span of fifteen to twenty years.[10] Clearly, crime reporting by journalists was not reflecting real crime trends. Instead, Sweden seemed, somewhat dazedly, to just wake up to the fact that racist and neo-Nazi ideologies could thrive even in affluent societies. There was a sense of failure in the attempt to integrate a growing immigrant population without friction. The media had become a platform for debates about crime, violence, and racial discrimination, as well as an arena for political moves by various stakeholders. In journalism's garish spotlight, the problems associated with crime became exaggerated—but at the same time, this reflected fears concerning contemporary developments that were real enough.

It is against this sociopolitical background that Stieg Larsson wrote his *Millennium Trilogy*. Mikael Blomkvist became his alter ego, the radical reporter who comes to grips with the horrors of the times.

The Journalist as a Crime Scriptwriter

In the years before and after the turn of the century, crime became a prominent issue for all political parties. In 2006, a center-right alliance won the Swedish elections, breaking a long period of social-democratic rule.[11] Concepts of deterrence and sentencing were central to criminal justice policy, continuing the trend from the 1990s. Several legislative amendments were made regarding penalties and the rights of crime victims. Mostly, it was a question of tougher sentencing, especially for crimes related to violence, drugs, and economics, and within the penal system there was a toughening of the measures of control over inmates.[12] The center-right alliance once again won the confidence of voters in the 2010 elections. The anti-immigrant Sweden Democrat Party, however, combining the ideas of an immigrant-free Sweden with a right-wing populist crime policy, was also voted into parliament.[13] For the first time in Swedish history, a party with a Nazi-influenced background was taking seats in parliament.[14]

Trends in the evolution of crime journalism in the early twenty-first century can best be summarized as *sensation, scandal, and spectacle*. Exceptional criminal cases receive considerable attention, particularly in the popular press and on commercial television. Yet the serious press and public-service television are also showing increasing interest. The media market has become highly commercialized, and the competition for consumers is fought with the help of crime stories.[15] The criminal is seen as "public enemy no. 1." At the same time, there is a certain glorification of the "crime hero" in the never-ending stream of exceptional crimes on display. Images of macho figures with pumped-up muscles and cool tattoos conjure up a world of fiction.

Following this trend are the documentary-style programs investigating crime. In many cases, it is difficult to determine whether the makers are serious or whether they are simply surfing on a wave of crime popularity, seeing an opportunity to grab an audience. "Infotainment," the genre somewhere between information and entertainment, is developing fast, with a wide selection available on different platforms. The Internet offers forums for discussions of crime: online news sites, blogs, and chat rooms. Sites supported by dubious political interests specialize in publishing the names and the images of suspected criminals at early stages of police investigations, while other sites track down previously convicted offenders in order to reveal their whereabouts. There is an ongoing debate among journalists and the general public about the influence these websites and social media have on the traditional media, which is seen to be moving in a more speculative and sensationalist direction.

In 2004, a murder drama took place in a Pentecostal congregation in the small Swedish village of Knutby, outside Uppsala. The entire congregation and community were depicted as the victims of an evil-minded pastor. The story is a striking example of how criminal acts are transformed into huge media spectacles. Through the police investigation and the journalists' reports, a series of remarkable power relations and sexual intrigues within the congregation were revealed.[16] The tragic events unfolded into endless popular entertainment, especially in the tabloid press and the gossip media. Within a few months, the extent of news reports on the case had widely surpassed media coverage of the assassination of the Swedish foreign minister Anna Lindh, which occurred in 2003. Knutby turned into a kind of reality show, with a stereotyped cast of characters. The combination of murder, sex, and sect provided food for the imagination and a whole series of books and documentaries about Knutby.

Meanwhile, during the last decade, the range of crime-based fiction has also expanded. There's a huge diversity of television crime programs of varying quality, some Swedish, but most American and British.[17] The market for crime literature is growing and seems nowhere near saturation. Swedish crime writers have been translated into a number of foreign languages, and many books have been made into movies, filmed both locally and abroad. In this context, it's not difficult to understand the massive success of *The Millennium Trilogy*.

One Hundred Cases of Deadly Violence

One important contribution made by media studies is the knowledge that there is no simple correlation between crime statistics and crime reporting. Most obviously, spectacular crimes and those linked with sex and violence are given priority, while the most common type of crime, property crime, is far less visible. Journalism is not a simple mirror of reality. Although juvenile crime rates in the 1990s were similar to those in the previous decade, crime reporting was strongly alarmist, and tougher measures were demanded.

Crime journalism may powerfully depict crime-related questions in a certain community at a certain moment in time—but this does not mean that crime is actually developing in the way portrayed by the media. Through sensationalist billboards and screaming headlines, journalists can easily mislead us into believing that the exceptional is the norm.

For the last thirty years in Sweden, there have been about a hundred cases of deadly violence per year, in the form of murder, manslaughter, and fatal assault. In the last fifteen years, this number has declined, particularly regarding victims under the age of fifteen. These numbers are not particularly dramatic for a population of approximately 9.4 million (2011).[18] In fact, Sweden is a fairly safe country by European standards, with an average crime rate on the same level as other West European states. Dramatic crime journalism may, however, give us a very different impression.

The fact that crimes get heavy media coverage can be explained from various angles. These stories fit the media's dramatic narrative style; they appeal to fundamental questions about human existence; they project much of the public's fear and anxiety onto scapegoats (the offenders) who are rarely able to defend themselves; they often allow for a moralizing twist; and they make good commercial business sense. Conditions governing news production decide what is given priority, together with situational factors such as ongoing debates and possible links to other stories and activities. What gets the spotlight is determined by the interplay between the media and its sources, comprising a variety of different players and stakeholders.

Serious investigative journalism has had a difficult time asserting itself in the first decade of this century. Economic pressures on newspapers, together with cuts in editorial staff, have led to dwindling resources for investigative work. Although the situation is nowhere near as drastic in Scandinavia as it is in the United States, the trend is the same. Electronic platforms and technological convergence have transformed the media landscape, and so have the public's media habits. These developments, however, involve contradictions: the public consumes media more selectively, and various channels are becoming more selective in their target groups, while, at the same time, certain events and phenomena have mass impact throughout the media landscape. Many of the news items that break through are reports of criminal activities.

In the Footsteps of Heroes

Fiction and reality blend in strange ways. The literary narratives of Blomkvist and Berger's *Millennium* magazine are manifested in the physical buildings, streets, and alleys that people visit in order to relive fictional events and crime scenes. The tales have real roots in the society where they were created and are therefore able to express something about contemporary life. Yet this doesn't mean that they correlate with events in the real world, on a factual level.[19] The question is: how do these literary tourists interpret the trilogy? When I'm asked, in my own neighborhood, where Mikael Blomkvist's editorial office is, I wonder how to answer.

Meanwhile, real crimes are being dramatized and fictionalized in a range of program formats that claim to reflect reality. The general public perceives an increased threat of crime, while politicians are regularly exposed to powerful public opinion as a result of exaggerated crime reporting. Frightened individuals are more inclined to accept populist demands for tougher policies. And sensationalist journalism based on flimsy evidence, creating an atmosphere of vigilante justice, is becoming increasingly common. The journalist who remains uncompromised, investigating the judicial system in the interests of the general public, describing criminal developments in order to make them comprehensible, is becoming increasingly rare. Where have you gone, Kalle Blomkvist?

NOTES

1. Stieg Larsson, *Män som hatar kvinnnor* (Stockholm: Norstedts, 2005), p. 500. My translation. Reg Keeland's translation leaves out important parts. See Stieg Larsson, *The Girl with the Dragon Tattoo*, trans. Reg Keeland (New York: Vintage, 2009), p. 514.

2. The historical evolution of crime journalism and criminal justice policy is based on a number of research studies, for example, Ester Pollack, *En studie i medier och brott* (*A Study in Media and Crime*) (Stockholm: JMK, Stockholms Universitet, 2001); and Ester Pollack, *Juvenile Crime and the Swedish Media in an Historical Perspective*, a series of contextualized, cross-sectional studies of the years 1955, 1975, and 1995 (Stockholm: JMK, Stockholm Media Studies, 2003).

3. Jerzy Sarnecki, *Introduktion till kriminologi* (*Introduction to Criminology*) (Stockholm: Studentlitteratur, 2009); and Hanns von Hofer and Henrik Tham, *Kriminologiska bidrag till Nationalencyklopedin 1989–1996* (*Criminological Contributions to the National Encyclopedia 1989–1996*) (Stockholm: Särtryck nr.23, Kriminologiska institutionen, Stockholms Universitet, 1996).

4. For example, see Sweden's biggest daily paper, *Dagens Nyheter* (*Daily News*), November 23, 1975.

5. During this decade, the role of the journalist as investigator of political power is formulated in a series of government inquiries; see, for example, Statens Offentliga Utredningar (SOU) 1975:78 *Svensk press. 3. Pressens funktioner i samhället.* 1972 års pressutredning (Stockholm, 1975) (Swedish Government Official Report 1975:78 *Swedish Press. 3. The Functions of the Press in Society.* 1973 Press report).

6. Special Bureau of the Defense Staff, known as the Information Bureau, was a secret undercover organization within the Swedish Armed Forces. One aim was to gather information about communists and other so-called security risks. It was exposed in 1973 by the journalists Jan Guillou and Peter Bratt. The affair became known as the IB affair. A public inquiry was published in 2002, SOU 2002:87. See also Jan Guillou's memoirs *Ordets makt och vanmakt. Mitt skrivande liv* (*The Power and Impotence of Words. My Writing Life*) (Stockholm: Piratförlaget, 2009), pp. 154–273.

7. Maj Sjövall and Per Wahlöö (1926–1975) wrote ten novels in the series *The Story of a Crime*, which have all been filmed, both in Sweden and abroad. The lead character is Inspector Martin Beck. He has also appeared in a series of new film adaptations, together with both old and new characters.

8. Several films have been based on Jan Guillou's books on intelligence officer Carl Hamilton. Apart from local productions, there have been Dutch and German adaptations. Guillou, *Ordets makt och vanmakt. Mitt skrivande liv*, (*The Power and Impotence of Words. My Writing Life*), pp. 417–429.

9. Another similarity is that both Guillou and Larsson write from a radical political perspective. This is also true of Henning Mankell, whose series of books about Wallander from the 1990s contributed to raising the status of Swedish crime fiction. Many new authors have followed, not least a series of women writers. See Jan-Erik Pettersson, *Stieg Larsson. Journalisten, författaren, idealisten* (*Stieg Larsson. Journalist, Author, Idealist*) (Stockholm: Telegram Bokförlag, 2010), pp. 185–212.

10. *Brottsutvecklingen i Sverige fram till år 2007* (*Crime in Sweden until the Year 2007*), Report 2008:23, Stockholm: Brå.

11. The winners of the election were Alliance for Sweden, a center-right coalition between the Moderate, Liberal, Center, and Christian Democrat parties. The prime minister, Fredrik Reinfeldt, belongs to the leading and largest party, the Moderates. Between 2006 and 2010, he led a majority government; after the 2010 election, a minority government.

12. Jerzy Sarnecki, *Brottsligheten och samhället* (*Crime and Society*) (Stockholm: Student-litteratur, 2010).

13. Issues concerning crime and immigration were prominent in the party's election campaign. The Sweden Democrats are one of the right-wing nationalist parties that Stieg Larsson investigated and wrote about in *Expo*, the magazine on which the *Millennium* is based. He predicted that one day the party would be accepted into polite political circles. See Pettersson, *Stieg Larsson. Journalisten, författaren, idealisten* (*Stieg Larsson. Journalist, Author, Idealist*), p. 149.

14. Since 1995, in Denmark the Danish People's Party, a conservative nationalist party, has helped fundamentally change Danish immigration policies in a more restrictive direction. In Norway, a similar right-wing populist party has operated since 1973, the Progress Party, and in Finland since 1995, the True Finns.

15. Ester Pollack, "Medier och brott" ("Media and Crime"), in Granhagen and Christianson, eds., *Handbok i Rättspsykologi* (*Handbook of Criminal Psychology*) (Stockholm: Liber, 2008).

16. The pastor's wife in a small Pentecostal congregation was murdered and a male neighbor badly wounded. The pastor was later convicted of incitement to murder, and a nanny who had previously worked for the family was convicted of murder and attempted murder.

17. In one week (February 2011), on the basic Swedish television cable network with ten channels (channels available to everyone), I counted more than fifty different program series about crime.

18. The Swedish National Council for Crime Prevention, *Dödligt våld* (*Fatal Violence*) (Stockholm: Brå, 2008).

19. For example, Sweden has never had a serial killer of female victims. Assault within close relationships is the most common type of violent crime involving women over the age of eighteen, accounting for 45 percent of police-reported cases. See *Anmälda brott. Preliminär statistik för 2010* (*Reported Crime. Preliminary Statistics for 2010*) (Stockholm: Brå, 2011).

PART THREE

STIEG LARSSON,
MYSTERY MAN

All the great artists were great workers, tireless not only in inventing, but also in rejecting, sifting, reshaping, ordering.

—Friedrich Nietzsche

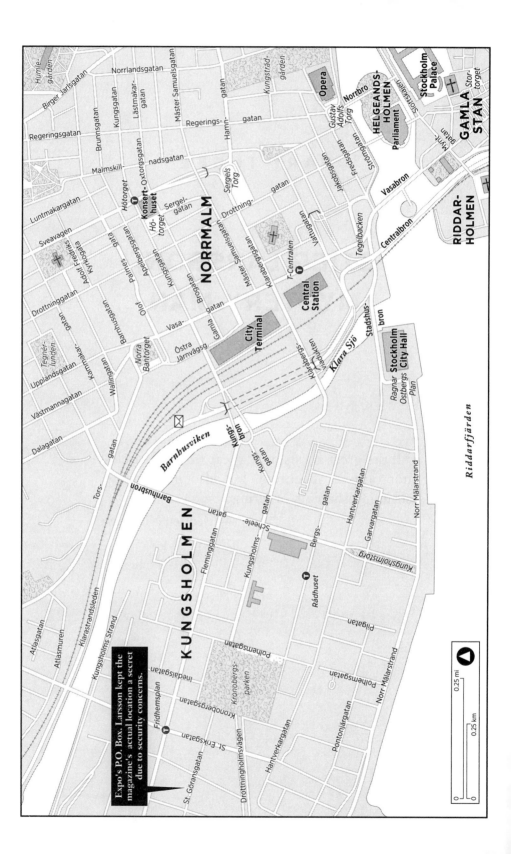

Expo's P.O. Box. Larsson kept the magazine's actual location a secret due to security concerns.

THE PHILOSOPHER WHO KNEW STIEG LARSSON: A BRIEF MEMOIR

Sven Ove Hansson

I first met Stieg Larsson on November 11, 1985. In a short note that I wrote to myself after the meeting, I concluded, "We seem to have quite a few puzzle pieces that fit together." Those puzzle pieces concerned information about extreme right-wing organizations in Sweden.

In those days, I split my time between Ph.D. studies in philosophy and freelance writing. Stieg was thirty-one years old and had worked since 1979 at Tidningarnas Telegrambyrå (TT), the largest news agency in Sweden. His main job was to provide illustrations such as maps and diagrams to accompany news articles. In addition, though, he wrote feature articles that covered a variety of subjects; some were overviews of recent crime novels (and are now interesting reference materials for those who wish to investigate his literary sources of inspiration). Yet this was not the reason that I was eager to meet him. I met him because of the investigations of Nazi, fascist, and

racist organizations that he undertook in his free time. Stieg
was also the Scandinavian correspondent of the British antifas-
cist magazine *Searchlight*.

We met many times in the late 1980s and the early 1990s
in cafés, sometimes at his workplace during nightshifts, sometimes at my place, and sometimes in the apartment he shared
with his wife, Eva Gabrielsson.[1] Because we were both night
owls, the meetings often took place late at night, with considerable amounts of coffee and, in his case, cigarettes.

Exposing Extremist Activities

Stieg was Sweden's leading figure in the investigation and exposure of racist organizations and their activities. Success in such
work depends on the time-consuming collection and analysis of
information from a wide variety of sources. Written documents
are essential. You have to collect newspaper clippings; the racists'
own journals, leaflets, and other publications; their candidate
tickets; and a wide range of other materials. Right-wing extremists are often interrogated by the police and appear before court.
(This applies not only to skinheads and uniformed Nazis but also
to racists in suits and ties who pose as respectable politicians.)
Therefore, documents from the police and courts of law are
often extremely useful. Additional information can be obtained
by taking notes and photographs at public meetings and by inter-
viewing members and ex-members. The law also leaves room for
other, less conventional means of collecting information, such as
infiltration and posing as a sympathizer when making inquiries.
By far the most important method, however, is patiently collecting and archiving large amounts of information and then
searching for patterns, such as when people from Nazi organizations appear in ostensibly respectable contexts.

Exchange of information is essential in laying out such puzzles. In the network of investigators, Stieg was always the best
informed, often able to locate and find the information that

others needed to complete their cases. He never seemed to have anything against others publishing material that was based on his own research; his aim was to have the Nazis and the racists exposed and their activities thwarted. He was also more than willing to provide respectable organizations with information they needed to avoid infiltration by racists. I corresponded with Stieg in 1993 about an organization that had such problems. Not surprisingly, he had all of the information that the CEO needed in order to assess the problem and decide how to deal with it.

Although Nazis and their like call themselves "national," they have a well-developed international network and often travel across borders for cooperation and inspiration. Among the Swedish extremism watchers, Stieg had a unique international overview that he shared generously with the rest of us. Better than anyone else, he spotted how extremists adopted messages and methods from their counterparts in other countries.

There are some similarities between private investigations of extremists and the intelligence work that the police under-take against the same groups. In both cases, the collection of large amounts of information is essential for revealing patterns and detecting trends. There are two big differences, how-ever. First, when serious crimes are suspected, the police have access to investigation methods such as phone tapping that are not available to private investigators. Second, police investi-gations are (and should be) restricted to criminal activities, whereas private investigators are free to dig into obnoxious but legally permitted forms of racism, xenophobia, homophobia, and discrimination. Of course, police and private investigators sometimes exchange information. Such contacts are usually respectful and frictionless, but now and then, some discord can arise. I am aware of one such case that involved Stieg. On October 17, 1989, he wrote to me,

> Your info that the gentlemen on Kungsholmen [the location of the police headquarters in Stockholm] have

asked X [another extremism watcher] to have a close look at the teacher in Bergslagen is most worrying. Anna-Lena and I have been working on that story for quite some time now, and Kungsholmen is aware of that. I do not at all like having such a crowd around Bergslagen since there is a risk that we run into each other and come under each other's feet. The result may be that a story we have been looking forward to with great interest will be lost. I think we should have a talk about this as soon as possible.[2]

After the Swedish prime minister Olof Palme was murdered in February 1986, there was much speculation concerning whether some extremist movement might be responsible for the murder. Extremism watchers were interviewed by the police in their search for clues and motives. In the first few weeks after the murder, Stieg was as preoccupied with it as the rest of us were. Three weeks after the murder, when I had for some reason been inaccessible by phone, he sent the following note to me:

I have phoned you dozens of times since the murder to hear if you have any hunch or ideas. I have a few myself but they have all turned into dead ends.[3]

Nonetheless, Stieg did not become one of the many private investigators who looked into the Palme murder. He knew too well that the crime could not be solved without the investigative resources that only the police have access to.

Stieg as a Writer

A few months before I first met Stieg, I had published a book on right-wing movements in Sweden.[4] One of the people who figured prominently in the book sued me for libel. That was unsurprising; litigation is a common method to discourage investigators. The lawsuit did not make me nervous because the book was entirely based on written documents that I could present in court. Yet I wanted to take the opportunity to present further facts that were embarrassing to the extremists. Stieg was able to provide me with documents that were most useful in the court proceedings, in particular, pertaining to connections between ostensibly respectable right-wing organizations in Sweden and outright Nazi organizations in other European countries. I would have won the trial regardless, but Stieg's help made the proceedings much more damaging to the plaintiff.

Two years later, in 1988, I introduced Stieg to Anna-Lena Lodenius, a young woman who had recently started to investigate right-wing extremism and who had access to very good sources that were complementary to Stieg's. Soon after they got to know each other, I proposed that they should join forces and write an overview of right-wing extremism in Sweden and elsewhere. I (easily) convinced a publisher and a friend of mine (Lars Hjalmarson) to support the project. The book, published three years later, provides an in-depth description of all of the major Nazi, fascist, and racist organizations in Sweden, along with an overview of international right-wing extremism. It is still considered the standard work in Swedish on the subject.[5]

I had the privilege of following the writing of this book very closely. I read and commented on all of the chapters at least twice, and I met Stieg and his coauthor many times during the process. Based not least on this experience, I am in a position to refute the claim that Stieg could not have written his novels himself because he was not a good enough writer. I received many pages directly from Stieg's typewriter (he was still using a typewriter at that time). On a few occasions, I was even present when he wrote. Stieg was an excellent writer with an unusual feel for dramaturgical structure. Like most good authors, he was grateful for comments and used them efficiently to improve his writing, often finding a third wording that was better than both his own original and my suggestion.[6]

Anti-Semitism as a Litmus Test

One of the many things I learned from Stieg is the importance
of recognizing signs of anti-Semitism in extremist writing
and propaganda. Of course, other forms of racism are equally
abominable, but anti-Semitism is a "litmus test" that almost
invariably reveals connections with Nazi and fascist movements. When you see anti-Semitism, dig deeper and often you
will find a lineage that leads all the way back to the NSDAP,
the German Nazi party.

In the decades following World War II, anti-Semitism
was seldom expressed in public, but since the late 1980s, it
has increasingly been voiced openly. As Stieg pointed out in
an article in 1998, anti-Semitism has regained its place as the
major theme in an increasing number of right-wing extremist
journals, pamphlets, and Web pages.[7] In another article, written two years later, he criticized local politicians in southern
Sweden who failed to clearly denounce expressions of anti-
Semitism in a demonstration against Israeli policies in which
they participated:

> To protest against the policies of the government of
> Israel is a self-evident right and it is just as legitimate
> as protesting on other occasions against the policies of
> the British, French, or Swedish government. But using
> such protests to attack a whole ethnic group—in this
> case the Jews—is classical anti-Semitism and has no
> place in a democratic context.[8]

Disclosing the Sweden Democrats

In 1979, Per Engdahl (1909–1994), a leading figure in Swedish
fascism since the 1920s, wrote an article in which he proposed
a new strategy for his movement. He had become convinced that
biological racism was no longer politically viable. He suggested,
therefore, that it be replaced by attacks on cultural differences

and immigration. In short, he proposed to use anti-immigrant rhetoric for the same purpose as previously racist rhetoric.[9] Three months later, a new organization, Bevara Sverige Svenskt (BSS, Keep Sweden Swedish) was formed, largely by veterans from his own and other fascist and Nazi groups. In 1988, this group was reorganized into a political party, Sverigedemokraterna (SD, the Sweden Democrats). Their early leadership was dominated by people with a background in openly Nazi and fascist organizations. Beginning in 1995, the party has attempted to clean its image by removing people with a fascist history from their lists of election candidates.[10] In the national elections in 2010, they obtained 5.7 percent of the votes, and they are now represented in the Swedish Parliament; however, their strategy is still the same as that outlined in Engdahl's article in 1979, namely, to use cultural arguments to attack the same groups that are attacked by biological arguments in traditional racism.

Stieg Larsson was among the first to recognize the new strategy of the Sweden Democrats—or, rather, to recognize that it was not new but adopted from other European extremists. The same strategy had been applied in Britain by the National Front, which was formed in 1967 with the fascist veteran A. K. Chesterton (1896–1973) as its first leader. Stieg wrote in 1991,

> It was Chesterton's strategy to create a movement against immigration that would seem sufficiently moderate to be able to give rise to a mass movement and attract the most reactionary elements on the right wing of the Tory party as a respectable alibi. He simply hoped to make racism respectable. This made it necessary—at least on the face of it—to keep the uniformed jerks at arm's length.[11]

This was exactly the same strategy that Engdahl outlined for Swedish right-wing extremism in 1979, and it is still applied by the Sweden Democrats and their counterparts in many other European countries today. Stieg saw this connection and its dangers earlier and more clearly than anyone else.

A Determined Democrat

Stieg's conviction was that it is the responsibility of democrats in general and democratic parties in particular to act against antidemocratic and racist extremism. The antiracist journal *Expo* that he was instrumental in starting in 1995 cooperated from the beginning with political youth organizations both to the left and to the right. As Stieg said in an interview,

> We must have democracy in full. Nazi and crazy fundamentalist groups have to be fought, but that should be done by democratic means.[12]

Sweden has a small organization of violent anarchists, Antifascistisk Aktion (AFA, Anti-Fascist Action), which fights right-wing extremists (and other political enemies) by violent means. In the same interview, Stieg said,

> Personally I have had a public debate with one of the leaders of AFA, and it became quite clear that I do not share their outlook or worldview. AFA is an extremely small movement but they receive 90% of the media attention. They have become almost synonymous with anti-racism. But the large anti-racist movement can be found in schools, among teachers, in the trade unions, among business owners and politicians.[13]

According to Stieg, an antiracist group that uses violence "could no longer call themselves an antiracist group and their whole idea would have been lost."[14]

Feminism and Honor Killings

Stieg was firmly opposed to all kinds of discrimination, not only the racist and xenophobic varieties. He wrote about homophobic violence and discrimination against women. One of his more ideological articles was an analysis of the notion of honor killing.[15] His starting point was very concrete. In early

2002, a young woman immigrant, Fadime Sahindal, was killed by her father, who could not accept her independent lifestyle. In the press, this was widely discussed as an example of an honor killing. It was considered part of a cultural pattern, and the murder was seen as causally connected to the fact that the murderer was an immigrant and a Muslim.

Three months earlier, another young woman, Melissa Nordell, had been murdered. She was killed by her boyfriend, who would not allow her independence. Neither she nor her boyfriend were immigrants, nor did they come from immigrant families. This murder was not treated as culturally determined or part of a "cultural pattern." Instead, it was described as an ordinary crime, that is, an exception to the culture, rather than something that follows from it. Yet this type of murder is more common among nonimmigrant Swedes than "honor killings" are among immigrants. So why were cultural explanations that put blame on a whole group used in almost all newspaper reports on the murder of Fadime Sahindal?

Although Stieg was not a philosopher, his text could be used in a philosophy seminar. Stieg's article used philosophical reasoning to reveal moral prejudices. He carefully analyzed two cases in order to determine what was similar and what differed between them. In doing so, he taught us an important lesson: the categories that we take for granted may lead us to draw the wrong moral conclusions.

Against Pseudoscience

Stieg and I had another interest in common: the exposure and refutation of pseudoscience. Two years before we first met, he had expressed his attitude about pseudoscience in a journal article:

> Recently I was introduced to a young lady in a café in Stockholm. The first question she asked after we had introduced ourselves was under what sign I was born.

She was in her thirties and I was later told that she had gone through primary school, secondary school and several years of university education. She has a progressive background and was a seemingly normal woman in full possession of all her senses. It is difficult to find an excuse why almost 500 years of enlightenment and scientific progress have failed so completely to leave any impression on her worldview.

The same as you, I said, that of the cow.

Then we said nothing more to each other. This was a brief acquaintance.

I may seem to be an unusually snooty person but it has started to irritate me that you can hardly cross the street without someone tapping your shoulder to ask under what sign you were born. A superstition that has been defunct since the days of Copernicus is a serious philosophy of life in 1983.[16]

In the same article, Stieg pointed out that superstitions such as astrology are often backed up with pseudoscientific arguments that are difficult for nonexperts to see through. Astrology "is just one example. Others are parapsychology, ufology, occultism, oriental mysticism, biorhythms, I Ching, numerology, pyramidology, chiromancy (fortune telling by looking at the hand), Atlantis cults, various forms of quackery, scientology and much else."[17]

Several of Stieg's feature articles for TT were entertaining and at the same time educative stories about myths and pseudosciences. One such article was based on James Randi's book *The Faith Healers*, which exposes some of the fraudulent methods used by so-called healers to create the illusion that they can cure diseases.[18] Another article recounted some recent discoveries on the Piltdown Hoax, the alleged remains of an early human that were found in 1912 but exposed as a forgery forty-one years later.[19] Yet another of his feature articles discussed various theories about a possible historical background for the Robin Hood myth.[20]

Although Stieg was very busy with his full-time job at TT and the work he did in his spare time exposing racists, he also helped the Swedish Skeptics, the Swedish organization for the defense of science against pseudoscience in which I was (and am still) active. In 1989, he wrote to me about the society's newsletter: "We must discuss the newsletter one of these days. . . . The way it looks it is much too thin and uninteresting."[21] If I remember correctly, this was followed by a very helpful conversation on how to improve the newsletter. On at least one occasion, he nominated an awardee for the society's yearly negative award.[22] He also generously contributed more than twenty drawings and a couple of photos for a book on pseudoscience that I published in 1986.[23]

Racist Pseudoscience

Stieg often emphasized that racism and xenophobia are largely based on pseudoscientific claims. Biological pseudoscience has a central role in racism, still to this day. Today historical revisionism, in particular, Holocaust denial, seems to be the most important pseudoscience in right-wing extremism. Stieg called historical revisionism an "icebreaker" for the resurgence of anti-Semitism in the 1990s.[24]

In 1989, the Swedish publishing company Legenda translated and published David Irving's biography of Göring. Irving had long been known for his pro-Nazi inclinations and had recently come out as a Holocaust denier. Stieg and I were both worried by this introduction of a pro-Nazi pseudoscientist in mainstream publishing. We cooperated in researching the issue. Stieg had material about Irving's pseudoscience and his Nazi connections close at hand from his British sources.[25] Not surprisingly, the Swedish publisher had previously published other forms of pseudoscience (related to UFOs).

We both agreed that the publisher's lax attitude concerning pseudoscience had paved the way for its mistake with the Göring book. A publisher that takes factual accuracy seriously would have consulted competent historians, who would have advised against publication. Our research and discussions gave rise to a sharp reaction from the Swedish Skeptics against the publication of Irving's book.[26]

This episode was also a major reason why we asked Stieg to write an article for the Skeptic newsletter about historical revisionism. In the article, which was published in 1990, he provided a short history of Holocaust denialism, exposed its close connections with fascism and neo-Nazism, and described and refuted its main claims (such as that the gas chambers did not exist, that Zyklon-B was used as a disinfectant, and other similar drivel). Of course, David Irving's activities and his connections with neo-Nazi and anti-Semitic organizations were also exposed.[27]

In another article several years later, Stieg returned to the topic of pseudoscience in right-wing extremism. After discussing Nazi racist biology, he pointed out that "since World War II the focus in these discussions has moved from traditional racial biology to fuzzier discussions on cultural differences between races and peoples. Just like before the claims are based on pseudoscience, but cultural differences are more difficult than genetic ones to define scientifically and this makes refutation more difficult."[28]

Stieg as a Skeptic

Stieg was a skeptic of the paranormal. He refused to believe the unsubstantiated claims of pseudoscience and mysticism, defended science as a road to knowledge, and rejected the "postmodern" idea that all of our knowledge is a social construction. He knew where relativism and irrationalism could lead. The Holocaust was not a social construction but an indisputable historical fact.

Stieg was also a rationalist, in the sense of believing in human rationality. Rationalism comes in several varieties. Stieg's rationalism was decidedly anti-elitist. He believed in changing society by providing the general public with facts and rational arguments. This, of course, had to take place in competition with irrational messages. Although basically an optimist, he was worried by the intensity with which irrational thought spread in society. The Internet did not make things easier. "With the Internet the lonely crackpot in a cellar has exactly the same means of distribution as the Swedish public radio and television. They have the same outreach and distribution. We have these irrational groups with the same penetrative power."[29] The only way to win the battle was with convincing arguments in a free and open debate.

Stieg also had another, somewhat more sophisticated argument against some of the common pseudosciences:

Astrology, for instance, promotes a deterministic worldview. It is typical for New Age spirituality that it makes propaganda for a view of the world that leaves no options for influencing the world through your own actions. This is a stifling form of spirituality, and in many cases self-fulfilling.[30]

This is an interesting argument not only against astrology but also against determinism in the philosophical sense. If we take determinism seriously in our own lives, then it gives us a reason to refrain from attempts to improve our own conditions and contribute to a better world. Stieg's idea that belief in determinism can be self-fulfilling is philosophically interesting and worthy of careful consideration.

Stieg as a Fiction Writer

I have written about the Stieg Larsson I knew, the fighter against racism and obscurantism. When reading his novels, I recognize much of the knowledge that he acquired through his investigations. In his studies of violent Nazi groups, he read numerous police reports and other legal documents describing murders and assaults. This explains the realism in his descriptions of violence. The investigative journalism described in the books has much in common with his own experience. And because he was always under threat, he had to be knowledgeable about personal security. Indeed, he would have been a competent staff member at Milton Security. (Actually, he wrote a handbook for threatened journalists, providing practical information about how to ward off various types of attack.)[31]

Racism watching is a puzzle-solving activity and often involves debunking pseudoscience. The investigator must try to figure out what makes people believe in weird ideas. As Stieg said in an interview, "[Fifty] years later people still believe in this, the whole neo-Nazi movement. There is absolutely no sense in this. They do it contrary to everything science tells us, contrary to human goodness or altruism, contrary to rational thinking. And this is fascinating. Why?"[32]

Many readers are—rightly—impressed by the enormous amount of detail that Stieg kept in mind and applied consistently in his trilogy, but I was already even more impressed by his ability to remember and combine an incredible amount of information about racist organizations. He seems to have been of the same opinion himself. In the only interview that he gave about his novels, he said, "It is easy to write crime novels. It is much more difficult to write an article of 5000 characters where everything should be one hundred percent correct."[33]

In a feature article for TT about the Tarzan books, he discussed why these books have been so successful:

> An important reason why the books are so popular is Tarzan's unique personality. He had no superpowers, no supernatural powers, but still he was not like any other human being.[34]

Today it is difficult to read these lines without thinking of Lisbeth Salander.

Stieg Larsson's ideas and convictions are clearly visible in his novels: his feminism and his contempt for discrimination, his conviction that hidden power structures should be brought to light, his anti-elitism, and, not least, his belief in the power of human rationality.

NOTES

1. I use the word *wife* because they were de facto husband and wife. As Eva has explained in a recent book, they chose not to marry in a formal sense. Stieg was living under threat, and a marriage entered into the civil registry would have made it much easier for violent extremists to track down his address (Eva Gabrielsson and Marie-Françoise Colombani, *Millennium, Stieg & jag* [Stockholm: Natur & Kultur, 2011], pp. 54–55). The first time that Stieg invited me to his home, he had to instruct me that the front-door nameplate said only "Gabrielsson."

2. Letter from Stieg Larsson to Sven Ove Hansson, 1989-10-17. In the author's possession.

3. Letter from Stieg Larsson to Sven Ove Hansson, 1986-03-20. In the author's possession.

4. Sven Ove Hansson, *Till höger om neutraliteten: bakom fasaden hos näringslivet och moderaterna* (Stockholm: Tiden, 1985).

5. Anna-Lena Lodenius and Stieg Larsson, *Extremhögern* (Stockholm: Tiden, 1991).

6. On the claim that he could not write, see also Eva Gabrielsson, "Min käre Stieg är ingen handelsvara," *Expressen*, January 31, 2010.

7. Stieg Larsson, "Antisemitismens återkomst," *Expo*, no. 3, 1998.

8. Stieg Larsson, "Judehatet—igen!" *Aftonbladet*, November 25, 2000. In another article in the same daily, he criticized an allegedly "culturally conservative" magazine that opened its pages for anti-Semitists and historical revisionists; Stieg Larsson, "Irving strör salt i aldrig läkta sår," *Aftonbladet*, July 7, 2000.

9. Per Engdahl, "Invandringens risker," *Vägen Framåt*, no. 3, April 1979.

10. Stieg Larsson, "Den 'nationella rörelsen'—historien om Sverigedemokraterna," in Richard Slätt, ed., *Sverigedemokraterna från insidan: berättelsen om Sveriges största parti utanför riksdagen* (Stockholm: Hjalmarson och Högberg, 2004), pp. 19–32.

11. Lodenius and Larsson, *Extremhögern*, p. 144.

12. Håkan Blomqvist, "Stieg Larsson. På barrikaden för demokratin," *Humanisten*, no. 3–4, 2002, pp. 40–43.

13. Ibid.

14. Stieg Larsson and Daniel Poohl, *Handbok för demokrater* (Stockholm: Expo, 2004), p. 83.

15. Stieg Larsson, "Svenskt och osvenskt våld mot kvinnor," in Stieg Larsson and Cecilia Englund, eds., *Debatten om hedersmord: feminism eller rasism* (Stockholm: Svartvitt, 2004), pp. 99–119.

16. Severin [pseudonym for Stieg Larsson], "Vidskepelsens världsbild," *Internationalen*, no. 39, 1983.

17. Severin, "Vidskepelsens världsbild."

18. Stieg Larsson, "Healing ren bluff," *Borås Tidning*, September 11, 1988; James Randi, *The Faith Healers* (Buffalo, NY: Prometheus Books, 1987).

19. Stieg Larsson, "Bluffen i Piltdown," *Östgöta Correspondenten*, September 8, 1994.

20. Stieg Larsson, "Robin Hood dikt eller verklighet," *Nya Wermlands-Tidningen*, January 5, 1989.

21. Letter from Stieg Larsson to Sven Ove Hansson, 1989-10-09. In the author's possession.

22. Undated letter from Stieg Larsson to Sven Ove Hansson, received in 1994. In the author's possession.

23. Sven Ove Hansson, *Förklarade mysterier* (Stockholm: Tiden, 1986).

24. Stieg Larsson, "Antisemitismens återkomst," *Expo*, no. 3, 1998.

25. Letter from Sven Ove Hansson to Stieg Larsson, 1990-03-11. Letter from Stieg Larsson to Sven Ove Hansson, 1990-03-19. Both in the author's possession.

26. "I lögnmakares sällskap" (editorial), *Folkvett*, no. 3–4, 1989, p. 3.

27. Stieg Larsson, "Antisemitismen med nytt ansikte," *Folkvett*, no. 2, 1990.

28. Stieg Larsson, "När rasister leker Gud," *Röd press*, 1997, 5:5–7.

29. Blomqvist, "Stieg Larsson. På barrikaden för demokratin."

30. Severin, "Vidskepelsens världsbild."

31. Stieg Larsson, *Överleva deadline—handbook för hotade journalister* (Stockholm: Svenska journalistförbundet, 2000).

32. Blomqvist, "Stieg Larsson. På barrikaden för demokratin."

33. Lasse Winkler, "En man för historieböckerna," *Svensk Bokhandel*, no. 18, 2004, pp. 12–13.

34. Stieg Larsson, "Hundra ljus i Tarzans tårta," *Hallandsposten*, July 16, 1988.

"THIS ISN'T SOME DAMNED LOCKED-ROOM MYSTERY NOVEL": IS *THE MILLENNIUM TRILOGY* POPULAR FICTION OR LITERATURE?

Tyler Shores

"The book is the pretext," Mikael Blomkvist remarks at the outset of his investigative assignment in *The Girl with the Dragon Tattoo*.[1] He is right. The Vanger family history is a cover story for his exploration into Harriet Vanger's disappearance decades ago. Yet *The Millennium Trilogy* is our own pretext to explore a larger question about our reading experience. Why do we read what we read?

There's also an important connection between the kinds of books we read and the kinds of reading we do. We seem to understand that when comparing Dostoyevsky's *Crime and Punishment* to Larsson's *The Girl with the Dragon Tattoo*, there is a qualitative difference between one as a literary work and the other as a work of popular fiction. But how do we go about deciding what the difference is between fiction and literature, if there even is one? And does it matter? Could it be that this distinction is made for us, well before we ever reach the pages of a book? We can use our experience of reading Larsson's crime novels to consider our own definition of literature and how we come to think of literature. Larsson has provided clues for us to think about his novels as more than merely crime fiction: "Because this isn't some damned locked-room mystery novel."[2] But if we know what such a book isn't, then what is it?

Popular Fiction and Locked Rooms: Why Do We Enjoy Mysteries?

Fiction is the domain of the possible, ranging widely from the impossible-to-be-true to the possibly true. Larsson's novels are this latter variety of realistic fiction, incorporating real-life settings in Sweden, actual people as characters (such as the boxer Paolo Roberto), and actual historical events (such as the assassination of Swedish prime minister Olof Palme in 1986).[3] Larsson's fictional Sweden includes fun layers of fictionality, such as a character within a crime novel reading a crime novel. During a lull in the action, Blomkvist reads a Val McDermid novel, *The Mermaids Singing*, to pass the time.[4] Not insignificantly, that novel is about a sadistic serial torturer and killer. "It was grisly," Blomkvist reflects.[5] Despite this fiction within fiction, there is an undeniably blunt reality to the novels. In *The Girl with the Dragon Tattoo*, each section of the book is prefaced with all-too-real statistics of crimes against women: "Forty-six percent of the women in Sweden have been subjected to violence by a man."[6] Larsson's Sweden may be fictional, but the crimes on which the novels are based are far from fiction.

As a particular type of fiction, the crime and detective novel genre attracts a good deal of literary interest. A possible reason for this, as Peter Brooks suggests, is that the very narrative structure of a detective novel is emblematic of what motivates us as readers: "the detective story [is] the narrative of narratives, its classical structure a laying-bare of the structure of all narrative."[7] In other words, when the characters seek out clues, piecing together information into a coherent whole, they mirror our own act of reading. As Blomkvist ruminates on a sensationalized murder case,

> The murder investigation was like a broken mosaic in which he could make out some pieces while others were simply missing. Somewhere there was a pattern. He could sense it, but he could not figure it out. Too many pieces were missing.[8]

Part of our pleasure in reading mysteries is that we find ourselves occupying the same position as the characters we are reading; in Larsson's puzzle-like plots, we, too, are fitting together the carefully parceled-out pieces of information as the story unfolds.

In this way, Larsson's novels become a perfect opportunity for philosophical thoughts on why we read. As much as we enjoy the thrill of reaching the end of a mystery, philosophy shows us that sometimes it's just as much about how we get there. Lisbeth Salander could perhaps make as good a philosopher as she does a detective: "She was not actually interested in the answer. It was the process of the solution that was the point."[9] There's something philosophically satisfying about the plot of the detective novel, in that the search for answers yields a tidy, definitive resolution. Laura Marcus suspects that one of the things that makes detective novels a particularly literary type of popular fiction is that they tend to have the kind of "narrative in which plot elements cohere and have meaning . . . ruled by chance and contingency in which the creation of a coherent story is a consolatory fiction."[10] Part of the consolation that we seek in fiction is a reassuring sense that truth can be found. This search is certainly a driving feature of the Larsson books: How did Harriet Vanger disappear? Who murdered Dag Svensson and Mia Johansson? Who was behind the Zalachenko cover-up? What was "All the Evil"? Unlike the clean resolution of some works of fiction, our real-life experience with the truth is never quite so tidy. As Alfred North Whitehead (1861–1947) once memorably remarked, "There are no whole truths; all truths are half-truths."[11]

While searching for truth, we notice that Larsson's characters read a wide range of books. Blomkvist indulges in mystery novels at Hedeby, Lisbeth reads *Dimensions in Mathematics* on the beaches at Grenada, and Inspector Monica Figuerola goes to bed reading about the idea of God in antiquity.[12] Likewise, our own various experiences of reading literature or popular fiction are based, to some extent, on our expectations of what we are going to read. Ken Gelder, in comparing the characteristic differences between popular fiction and literature, wrote,

> The reader of popular or genre fiction, however, is an "addict" who "devours" one work after another. There is no re-reading here: once a work has been read, it is put aside and the reader moves on to the next generic example (or, perhaps, the next novel in the series).[13]

Given the serial nature of popular fiction, its readers might be said to read horizontally, eager to get to the end of one book and into the next in a series or into the next author within a genre.

We can see how the serial nature of fiction works within Larsson's novels—each book in some sense can function as a stand-alone reading experience, but they're most enjoyable when read as one long story. Readers of literature, on the other hand, tend to read vertically, reading slowly for depth of meaning. And just as we might say that readers have certain expectations of literature, literature has expectations of its readers. Friedrich Nietzsche (1844–1900), a particularly literary philosopher, described his ideal reader in *Ecce Homo*: "When I try to picture the character of a perfect reader, I always imagine a monster of courage and curiosity, as well as of suppleness, cunning, and prudence—in short, a born adventurer and explorer."[14]

War of the Words: Fiction with a Purpose

Larsson, himself a voracious reader of crime and detective fiction, includes several references to Swedish fiction within his novels. That Blomkvist finds three novels by the Swedish writer Astrid Lindgren on a bookshelf is significant because Larsson the crime novelist drew part of his inspiration from two of Lindgren's most popular fictional characters: Pippi Longstocking and Kalle Blomkvist (which serve as teasingly diminutive nicknames for Lisbeth and Blomkvist, respectively).[15] Rather than seek a definition of what literature *is*, we might be better off with a definition by approximation, such as the philosopher Ludwig Wittgenstein's (1889–1951) "family resemblances" of complex concepts.[16] Our understanding of literature is shaped in comparison to other similar type of works. There is a decidedly subjective element to all of this, and, ultimately, "Literature means different things to different people."[17]

One thing that literature means to readers is its capacity to deal with "moral seriousness . . . an aspiration to tackle broad human concerns."[18] Some of the issues Larsson addresses in his novels unmistakably fall under the category of moral seriousness: violence toward women, government corruption, journalistic ethics, to name a few. Such writing, according to French philosopher Jean-Paul Sartre (1905–1980), is a "committed literature" with the intention of social commitment, advocating or inspiring real, political, and positive change in the world.[19] Perhaps what differentiates Larsson's novels from other forms of popular genre fiction is that he chooses to present "a thoroughly ugly view of human nature."[20] When the depth of Martin Vanger's murderous history is fully revealed in *The Girl with the Dragon Tattoo*, Blomkvist is left helplessly to ask, "Why?" Vanger's chillingly simple response speaks volumes of Larsson's views on such invisible crimes: "Because it's so easy."[21]

That the novels are collectively called *The Millennium Trilogy* emphasizes the central role of journalism and writing as a means toward truth and its capacity to serve as an agent of social change, emphasizing the "theme of how words can be a force for justice."[22] Taken as a whole, the trilogy grows from detective novel into something more. The bad guys range widely from murderers, sex traffickers, bikers, and corrupt businessmen to corrupt politicians, corrupt cops, and clandestine Cold War–era government agents. Blomkvist, a fictional analogue of Larsson and Larsson's own lifelong crusade of investigative crime reporting, is at one point ironically described by Lisbeth as "An insufferable do-gooder who thought he could change everything with a book."[23]

Larsson's novels also have an uncompromising moral purpose, as Blomkvist reiterates at the conclusion of the trilogy: "When it comes down to it, this story is not primarily about spies and secret government agencies; it's about violence against women, and the men who enable it."[24] When we reflect on the reasons why we read, we might consider the following question: Is reading a form of escapism, a respite from our (occasionally) banal real-world existence into a fictional one that's more exciting? Or do we read in order to better understand and thus engage with the world in which we live? [25]

What we read inevitably has a certain applicability to our lived experiences: "Literary fictions, it can be argued, can not only increase our knowledge and understanding of the real world, but also contribute more directly to our ability to engage with that world, and with other human agents, in ways that contribute to our individual and collective good."[26]

Contemporary philosopher Martha Nussbaum, in discussing the ways in which fiction and literature can enhance our capacity for moral reasoning, wrote that reading provides "not simply intellectual grasp of propositions; it is not even simply intellectual grasp of particular facts; it is perception. It is seeing a complex concrete reality in a highly lucid and richly responsive way; it is taking in what is there, with imagination and feeling."[27] Fiction can help us cultivate our capacity for such moral reasoning by depicting complex emotions and human failings that we encounter in our own lives. Lisbeth, for instance, with her characteristically black-and-white form of morality, blames Harriet Vanger for not preventing her brother Martin's decades-long murderous spree.

> "Bitch," she said.
>
> "Who?"
>
> "Harriet Fucking Vanger. If she had done something in 1966, Martin Vanger couldn't have kept killing and raping for thirty-seven years."
>
> "Harriet knew about her father murdering women, but she had no idea that Martin had anything to do with it. She fled from a brother who raped her and then threatened to reveal that she had drowned her father if she didn't do what he said."
>
> "Bullshit."[28]

Should we consider Harriet morally culpable for her brother's later crimes? Or should we consider her a victim? Fiction encourages us to use our imagination, to empathize, and to take that conceptual leap between the characters and potentially our own selves, to imagine "what it is like to be a certain sort of character or in a certain sort of predicament."[29]

Empathizing with characters is an emotional investment on our part. We have very real emotional/psychological responses to fictional events that we know are not real. Philosophers call this the "paradox of fiction." The paradox raises this question: Must we believe that something or someone actually exists in order to be emotionally moved? For that matter, why would we care about something that isn't real? Do we simply engage in a "willing suspension of disbelief," as the English poet Samuel Taylor Coleridge (1772–1834) called it? Part of the appeal of Larsson's novels is the complexity of Lisbeth Salander's character. For all of her apparent toughness, she is also an emotionally vulnerable social outsider exploited by others. Perhaps, in fictional characters, with all of their complexity, contradictions, and all-too-human failings, we may see a reflection of, and a resemblance to, ourselves.

It's All Relative: Culture, Fiction, and Literature

The experience of reading occurs within ourselves; it is a transaction between a person and the printed words of a book. Yet cultural factors inevitably play small, often imperceptible roles in the ways we come to our understanding of literature and popular fiction:

> [B]ookshops, libraries, publishers' catalogues, literary festivals and prizes, reviewing in mass-media outlets, reading and adaptations on radio, tv, and film, all constantly reinforce the acquisition of "literary competence."[30]

Stanley Fish, in his book *Is There a Text in This Class?* suggests that this could be a collectively made decision; how things are read will mean different things within different communities of readers. In some ways, the question is a classic chicken-or-the-egg situation: Is a work of fiction considered to be literature because we bring to it certain literary expectations, or is it literature only after we recognize and read it as such?

Critical attention is one of those cultural practices that contributes to our collective understanding of literature. In "The Critic as Artist," Oscar Wilde (1854–1900) observed that critics are positioned as the cultural authorities to determine literary value, but such authority is also paradoxically dependent on the very things that they seek to criticize. Critical scrutiny becomes a tricky barometer for our own reading of Larsson's novels. As a reviewer for the *New Yorker* observed, "We're not looking at Tolstoy here."[31] No, we're not. But so what? We love the Larsson novels for being great, enthralling stories, but at the same time they include their fair share of improbable coincidences and lists of exhaustive details (such as a complete description of Lisbeth's IKEA purchases and the arrangement of said furniture in *The Girl Who Played with Fire*). Depending on whom you ask, this meticulous description is either an attempt to capture the minute details of real life or a classic example of too much information. And yet somehow we suspect that literature means more to us than simply a well-written turn of phrase.

This leads us to a more broadly philosophical question about culture—namely, the differentiation between the so-called high and low cultures. The British cultural critic Matthew Arnold (1822–1888) popularized arguments about high and low culture by decrying the failures of high culture that he perceived had led to an "anarchy" of low culture (what we today call popular culture). The notion of high and low culture is a complex, socially constructed distinction; something that both creates a culture's prevailing ideology and is created by it:

> The literary work's authority derives sometimes from the belief that the work is an accurate representation of social reality and its reigning ideological assumptions. . . . Sometimes the conferred authority derives from a belief that literature shapes social structures and beliefs.[32]

Yet if literature becomes associated with Arnold's high culture, it would seem that literature can be defined only in a negative sense; that it needs something such as popular fiction in order to define itself. As Perry Meisel notes in *The Myth of Popular Culture*, a better argument might be a dialectical relationship between "high" and "low" to produce a "middle" culture. "The relation of high and low, the learned and the popular, is not hierarchical. The popular—the low—and its literary representative—the presumably high—are actually on a level field."[33] When we consider fiction such as *The Girl with the Dragon Tattoo*, it seems as if there is something else we're interested in. "The prose is not the point."[34]

Perhaps the point is not an either/or proposition but instead a matter of distinguishing between varying shades of gray, to realize that "works which are not literary works at all may yet have literary qualities, good or bad."[35] All works of literature have social value. They also have, to varying degrees, an entertainment and a commercial value. Larsson, tired from his longtime struggles with keeping his magazine *Expo* afloat financially, had hoped that his crime novels would be his "retirement fund."

The *Millennium* books are unlikely best-sellers, yet by the middle of 2010, their success had become a phenomenon. Even the term *best-seller* is itself telling—almost as if to imply that the value of a work of fiction or literature is regarded by its commercial success: *if other people are buying it, you should buy it, too.*

Stieg Larsson and the Girl Who Redefined Crime Fiction?

Larsson's novels, as popular fiction, are unusual for their steadfast focus on morality and social consciousness. Heather O'Donoghue, a crime fiction critic for the *Times Literary Supplement*, reflects on the combination of factors from which Larsson's novels draw their appeal:

> The root of Larsson's success lies in his combination of serious literary virtues—his novels are well written, well

plotted, with very original, finely drawn characters and a meticulous, credible analysis of modern society— and his very basic, exciting and even visceral appeal to the reader's emotions: terror, pity, moral outrage and the fundamental thrill of right at last overcoming wrong.[36]

We recognize the Larsson books as crime and detective novels, yet somehow, crucially, they seem to be more than that. It's not enough for Larsson to have the crimes solved. The social corruption behind those crimes must be revealed: "The whodunit becomes the exposé."[37] Perhaps in this way Larsson's novels provide an example of what is possible in his genre, a kind of socially conscious popular fiction. The world that Larsson creates in his fictional Sweden is filled with crime and grisly violence, yet it's essentially a message of optimism; there is corruption in the world, but it's fixable.

The dividing line between fiction and literature is often hard to distinguish, and such vagueness is not necessarily a bad thing. Fiction and literature are ways to supplement our own lived experiences. While Oscar Wilde famously observed that "Life imitates Art far more than Art imitates Life," sometimes the two can and do intersect. We read in order to have a further understanding of life and the people around us, which in turn gives us a better understanding of what we read. Like literature, good fiction can help change the ways in which we view our world. Larsson's crime fiction is Exhibit A.

NOTES

1. Stieg Larsson, *The Girl with the Dragon Tattoo*, trans. Reg Keeland (New York: Vintage, 2009), p. 87.

2. Ibid., p. 502.

3. Fans of the novels can now even take walking tours of Larsson's Sweden, including the 7-Eleven store that sells Lisbeth's crime-fighting food of choice: Billy's Deep Pan Pizzas ("The Real Story behind Stieg Larsson and *The Girl with the Dragon Tattoo*," *Sunday Times*, May 2, 2010).

4. Interestingly enough, Blomkvist's choice of crime fiction reading takes its title from a literary work: T. S. Eliot's literary poem "The Love Song of J. Alfred Prufrock" ("I have heard the mermaids singing, each to each").

5. Larsson, *The Girl with the Dragon Tattoo*, p. 363.

6. Ibid., p. 127.

7. Peter Brooks, *Reading for the Plot: Design and Intention in Narrative* (Cambridge, MA: Harvard University Press, 1992), p. 25.

8. Stieg Larsson, *The Girl Who Played with Fire*, trans. Reg Keeland (New York: Vintage, 2010), p. 454.

9. Ibid., p. 27.

10. Laura Marcus, "Detection and Literary Fiction," in Martin Priestman, ed., *The Cambridge Companion to Crime Fiction* (New York: Cambridge University Press, 2003), p. 260.

11. Alfred North Whitehead, *Dialogues of Alfred North Whitehead*, ed. Lucien Price (Jaffrey, NH: David R. Godine, 2001), p. 14.

12. Ironically enough, in a novel filled with references to fiction, it's the *Dimensions in Mathematics*, supposedly written by L. C. Parnault, that ends up being a nonexistent fictional book—a fact that Harvard University Press would go on to address on its blog, http://harvardpress.typepad.com/hup_publicity/2009/02/dimensions-in-mathematics-a-phantom-a-chimera.html.

13. Ken Gelder, *Popular Fiction: The Logics and Practices of a Literary Field* (New York: Routledge, 2004), p. 41.

14. Friedrich Nietzsche, *On the Genealogy of Morals and Ecce Homo*, trans. Walter Kaufmann (New York: Vintage, 1989), p. 36.

15. Something both characters resent, as Lisbeth notes,
"Kalle Blomkvist."
"He hates the nickname, which is understandable. Somebody'd get a fat lip if they ever called me Pippi Longstocking" (Larsson, *The Girl with the Dragon Tattoo*, p. 51).

16. Ludwig Wittgenstein, *Philosophical Investigations*, trans. P. M. S. Hacker and Joachim Schulte (Oxford: Wiley-Blackwell, 2009).

17. Peter Widdowson, *Literature* (New York: Routledge, 1999), p. 10.

18. Peter Lamarque, *The Philosophy of Literature* (Malden, MA: Blackwell, 2009), p. 32.

19. Interestingly enough, Sartre himself was awarded but declined the Nobel Prize for Literature in 1964.

20. Alex Berenson, "Book Review: The Girl with the Dragon Tattoo," *New York Times*, September 14, 2008.

21. Larsson, *The Girl with the Dragon Tattoo*, p. 447.

22. Kate Mosse, "Review: The Girl Who Kicked the Hornet's Nest," *Guardian*, October 3, 2009.

23. Larsson, *The Girl Who Played with Fire*, p. 603.

24. Stieg Larsson, *The Girl Who Kicked the Hornet's Nest*, trans. Reg Keeland (New York: Alfred A. Knopf, 2010), p. 514.

25. Larsson, in an e-mail to his editor: "A rule of thumb has been never to romanticize crime and criminals, nor to stereotype victims of crime. I base my serial murderer in book I on a composite of three authentic cases. Everything described in the book can be found in actual police investigations" (Stieg Larsson, *On Stieg Larsson*, trans. Laurie Thompson [New York: Knopf, 2010], p. 14).

26. David Davies, *Aesthetics and Literature* (London: Continuum, 2007), p. 164.

27. Martha Nussbaum, *Love's Knowledge: Essays on Philosophy and Literature* (New York: Oxford University Press, 1990), p. 152.

28. Larsson, *The Girl with the Dragon Tattoo*, p. 499.

29. Lamarque, *The Philosophy of Literature*, p. 244.

30. Widdowson, *Literature*, p. 100.

31. Joan Acocella, "Why Do People Love Stieg Larsson's Novels?" *New Yorker*, January 10, 2011, pp. 70–74.

32. J. Hillis Miller, *On Literature* (New York: Routledge, 2002), p. 100.

33. Perry Meisel, *The Myth of Popular Culture: From Dante to Dylan* (Malden, MA: Wiley-Blackwell, 2010), p. 18.

34. Charles McGrath, "The Afterlife of Stieg Larsson," *New York Times*, May 20, 2010.

35. Christopher New, *Philosophy of Literature* (New York: Routledge, 1999), p. 3.

36. Barry Forshaw, "The Real Story behind Stieg Larsson and *The Girl with the Dragon Tattoo*," *Sunday Times*, May 2, 2010.

37. Ian MacDougall, "The Man Who Blew Up the Welfare State," *n + 1*, February 27, 2010, http://nplusonemag.com/man-who-blew-up-welfare-state.

WHY WE ENJOY READING ABOUT MEN WHO HATE WOMEN: ARISTOTLE'S CATHARTIC APPEAL

Dennis Knepp

Imagine a story about a young woman named Lisbeth Salander who grows up in a loving family with supportive parents who recognize her unusual mathematical genius and do their best to nurture it. Caring and humane psychologists diagnose the young Salander as having Asperger's syndrome and instruct her devoted family on ways to properly care for her. Suppose that Salander becomes a great computer programmer whose genius is used to develop a cure for cancer. In this alternate narrative, the adult Lisbeth Salander is still considered unable to handle her own finances (she is a mathematical genius, but she can't balance her own checkbook—which would be quaint and quirky in this nicer narrative), but her financial guardian is a good man who helps Salander buy expensive computers.

We can imagine all of these things, but (yawn) we can't imagine reading a book about it. The alternative narrative sounds completely boring. We much prefer a narrative in which Salander's guardian, Herr Advokat Nils Bjurman, punches her in the face, handcuffs her to his bed, and repeatedly rapes her. The scene is so violent and grotesque that even the judge cannot bear to watch it during the court proceedings and asks that the DVD be stopped. Why, then, do we read all of the graphic details? Why do we prefer to read the disturbing narrative, rather than a nicer alternative?

"Bring Me the Man-Killing Ax!"

The philosopher Plato (428–348 BCE) witnessed the flourishing of theater in ancient Athens with its two forms of art: tragedy and comedy. It's obvious why people like comedies—it feels good to laugh. The ancient comedies of Aristophanes (446–386 BCE) are still funny today—especially his sex comedy, *Lysistrata*. But why did the ancient Athenians love tragedies?

Consider the story of *Agamemnon* by Aeschylus (524–455 BCE). King Agamemnon has just returned from ten years of fighting the Trojan War. He survives the sacking of Troy and the treacherous return voyage, only to be killed by his unfaithful wife, Clytaemnestra, on his very first day home. She welcomes him with exaggerated flattery, gets the king to strip off his armor and weapons to take a bath, and slaughters her naked husband with an ax.[1] In ancient Greek art, Clytaemnestra is always shown with a two-headed battle ax. Salander axing her father in the climactic scene of *The Girl Who Played with Fire* is part of an ancient tradition of powerful women killing their abusive male kin with this weapon of choice, although Salander must make due with a wood-chopping ax. In *The Libation Bearers* (Aeschylus's sequel to *Agamemnon*), Clytaemnestra shouts to her servants, "Bring me the man-killing ax!"[2] Yet after receiving her battle ax, Clytaemnestra is killed by her own son, Orestes, who is avenging his father's death. And you thought the Vangers were a dysfunctional family!

Plato argued in his *Republic* that this kind of disturbing violence should be censored because people imitate what they see. If people watch scenes of bad behavior, then they will learn to do bad things. If people watch scenes of good behavior, they will learn to do good things. Perhaps Plato would have preferred Aeschylus to write a trilogy in which King Agamemnon returns victorious from the Trojan War to find his faithful wife, Clytaemnestra, there with their happy children, Orestes and Electra. Similarly, maybe Stieg Larsson should write a trilogy in which Zalachenko defects to Sweden as an informant and is a good husband to his wife and a good father to their two daughters. I hope that Plato is wrong, because the story about Zalachenko as a family man sounds incredibly boring.

Aristotle's Catharsis

Aristotle (384–322 BCE), Plato's most famous student (and, in many ways, his rival), believed that there is value in disturbing stories. In his *Poetics*, Aristotle wrote about how tragic heroes need to be exaggerations of ourselves so that we may see their characteristics more clearly. Tragic heroes cannot be godlike, for then we would never see ourselves in them. They should be less than perfect so that we can sympathize with their plight and put ourselves in their shoes. Lisbeth Salander is such a character. She is an exaggeration, but she is not godlike. Lisbeth is a fallible human, and her character flaws often put her into dangerous situations.

Salander's exaggerated character allows us to see her flaws more clearly, and her flaws let us identify with her. According to Aristotle, our identification with Salander is crucial because it enables us to feel both pity and terror. We feel pity and compassion for her because she does not deserve to suffer; we also feel terror in our recognition that we are like her, so we, too, could suffer a similar fate.[3] Because Salander is an exaggerated character, we can see this more clearly. We can see that her intense hatred for authority figures puts her into a situation in which Bjurman can attack her without worrying that she will notify the authorities. What Salander thinks of as defiant independence, we can see as recklessness. We feel pity and compassion when Bjurman attacks her because no young woman deserves to suffer so horribly, and we feel terror because we can imagine a kind of powerlessness that puts us all in potentially dangerous situations.

Aristotle wrote that we achieve "by means of pity and terror a catharsis of such emotions."[4] There is debate among Aristotle scholars over the meaning of this word *catharsis*. For centuries, the traditional understanding of catharsis has been a "purging."[5] The analogy here is with ancient medical practices. In the ancient world, physicians didn't have access to medicines such as penicillin, antibiotics, and aspirin. They didn't even know about germs. Ancient physicians believed that you had to get the bad stuff out of a person in order to heal him or her. So doctors would prescribe vomiting, diuretics, and bleeding in order to purge the bad stuff out of a sick person. This purging was described as a "catharsis." For Aristotle, the analogy seems to be that watching or reading disturbing scenes enables us to achieve a purgation of the dangerous emotions of pity and terror. Afterward, we feel better for having vomited out these emotions.

For a different example, think about a heavy metal concert. I have attended many heavy metal concerts (Slayer is my favorite!), and I always return home slightly damaged. My ears will ring for days, my neck hurts from head-banging, my feet hurt from stomping, my voice is shot, and sometimes I get nasty bruises from crashing into other concertgoers. I would have paid money to see Salander's friends in Evil Fingers and worn the T-shirt, too. But why would I intentionally put myself into a harmful situation? Because I get to experience anger in a relatively safe environment so that afterward I feel less angry. I get to shout violent lyrics without actually experiencing any real violence. A heavy metal concert is like a roller-coaster ride: all of the thrills of danger without the danger. By experiencing some anger, I am able to purge myself and feel less angry.

Although it makes some sense to purge anger, the catharsis/ purgation theory assumes that it is good to purge our emotions of pity, compassion, terror, and fear as well. This is a strange theory. A person without compassion or fear would be a monster like Ronald Niederman. When Niederman kidnaps Miriam Wu, brings her to an abandoned warehouse, beats her up, and threatens to cut off her limbs with a chainsaw, he has no pity for her cries for mercy. He has no compassion. When the professional boxer Paolo Roberto shows up at the warehouse to save Miriam Wu and begins punching Niederman in the face, the monster has no fear. He has no feeling of terror. If Aristotle's theory advocates creating unfeeling monsters such as Niederman, then we have to reject it. To suggest that art turns people into monsters is basically to suggest that art is bad for you. So, we're back to Plato's idea that artists should write only good stories with good characters doing good things. We're back to boring art.

Nussbaum's Clarification

The eminent Aristotle scholar Martha Nussbaum proposes a different interpretation of Aristotle's catharsis. According to Nussbaum, catharsis is used metaphorically in medicinal contexts. Originally, catharsis meant "clarification or cleaning up." Nussbaum provides examples of catharsis as "water that is clear and open, free of mud and weeds; of a space cleared of objects; of grain that is winnowed, and so clear of chaff; of the part of an army that is not functionally disabled or impeded; and, significantly and often, of speech that is not marred by some obscurity or ambiguity."[6] In medicine, when an ancient Greek physician prescribed a purgative or a diuretic to rid your body of unhealthy bile, it was a catharsis because it was a clarification or a cleaning up of your health. Equipped with this understanding of catharsis/clarification, Nussbaum creates a better understanding of Aristotle's theory: "the function of a tragedy is to accomplish, through pity and fear, a clarification (or illumination) concerning experiences of the pitiable and fearful kind."[7] When Aristotle wrote that Athenians watching a Greek tragedy had a catharsis of the emotions of pity and fear, it meant that the audience came to a better understanding of these emotions. Art is educational.

The ancient Athenians watching Aeschylus's *Agamemnon* would understand how the gods can give contradictory demands that destroy good men.[8] This isn't a purgation of fear so that we become fearless. This is an understanding of fear—the world is a confusing place, and art can serve to clarify and dispel our confusion.

Equipped with the catharsis/clarification theory, we can return to Bjurman's horrifying rape of Lisbeth. The world is a dangerous and confusing place where horrible rapes of young women happen all too frequently. Larsson starts part 2 of *The Girl with the Dragon Tattoo* with this chilling epigram: "Forty-six percent of the women in Sweden have been subjected to violence by a man."[9] This is not only a statistic in a report, a factoid read by few. In Larsson's trilogy, millions of people read in chilling detail how such things can happen. It is a function of power. Bjurman is Salander's guardian. In his discussion of guardianship, Larsson wrote, "Taking away a person's control of her own life—meaning her bank account—is one of the greatest infringements a democracy can impose, especially when it applies to young people."[10] Bjurman justifies the rape: "She had to understand who was in charge."[11] Later the serial rapist Martin Vanger describes "the godlike feeling of having absolute control over someone's life and death."[12] Vanger is a man of wealth and power who preys on women who have neither. As a result of reading the trilogy, we can understand that men who hate women use their power and authority to abuse helpless young women. We can understand the dangers of the guardianship program. We can better understand the relationship between rape and power. We have a better understanding of our pity for Salander—she does not deserve this abuse from a man who has been assigned to help her. And we have a better understanding of our own fears—we could find ourselves in a situation in which someone else has absolute power over us and abuses that power. Reading Larsson's trilogy is educational, even inspirational. We get it. We can be moved to do something about it. We can work to make a world in which young women are not under the absolute authority of a single man.

Salander's Satisfying Revenge

The ancient tragedies sure don't come with happy endings! Aeschylus wrote about Clytaemnestra killing Agamemnon. Sophocles (497–406 BCE) wrote about King Oedipus unknowingly killing his own father and marrying his mother. Euripides (480–406 BCE) wrote about Queen Medea killing her own children.

By contrast, Salander gets her revenge. On her next visit to Bjurman, Salander knocks him out with a Taser, strips him naked, and ties him up spread-eagled. Bjurman knows that the power has shifted: "*She had taken control.*"[13] She tattoos I AM A SADISTIC PIG, A PERVERT AND A RAPIST on his chest. Cruel, but doesn't Bjurman deserve it? Aristotle wrote that watching "a thoroughly villainous person falling from good fortune into misfortune" is not tragic but "can contain moral satisfaction."[14] And Salander's revenge is certainly satisfying.

NOTES

1. Aeschylus, "Agamemnon," in *Oresteia*, trans. Peter Meineck (Indianapolis: Hackett, 1998).

2. Aeschylus, "The Libation Bearers," in *Oresteia*, p. 105.

3. See Richard Janko's glossary for his translation of *eleos* as "pity" and *phobos* as "terror" in Aristotle's *Poetics* (Indianapolis: Hackett, 1987), pp. 217 and 224.

4. Aristotle, *Poetics*, trans. Richard Janko (Indianapolis: Hackett, 1987), 49b27, p. 7.

5. See Richard Janko's glossary for *catharsis* on page 200 and in his introduction on pages xvi–xx. For a similar analysis, see the entry for "*katharsis*: purgation, purification," in F. E. Peters, *Greek Philosophical Terms: A Historical Lexicon* (New York: New York University Press, 1967), pp. 98–99. After discussing the use of *katharsis* in ancient medical practices, Peters wrote regarding Aristotle's use of the term: "Aristotle took the further step and incorporated it into his theory of art, with the well-known result of tragedy's being defined in terms effecting a homoeopathic *katharsis*/purgation of the *pathe* of pity and fear (*Poet.* 1449b)," p. 98. Notice that Peters calls this "well-known."

6. Martha Nussbaum, *The Fragility of Goodness: Luck and Ethics in Greek Tragedy and Philosophy*, updated edition (New York: Cambridge University Press, 2001), p. 389.

7. Nussbaum, *The Fragility of Goodness*, p. 391.

8. See Nussbaum's "Chapter 2: Aeschylus and Practical Conflict," in *Fragility of Goodness*, pp. 25–50, on the contradictory demands of the Greek gods and how this leads to Agamemnon's tragic downfall.

9. Stieg Larsson, *The Girl with the Dragon Tattoo*, trans. Reg Keeland (New York: Vintage, 2009), p. 127.

10. Ibid., p. 225.

11. Ibid., p. 246.

12. Ibid., p. 448.

13. Ibid., p. 258.

14. Aristotle, *Poetics*, 53a1–3, page 16.

THE DRAGON TATTOO
AND THE VOYEURISTIC
READER

Jaime Weida

The Millennium Trilogy contains all of the elements of successful crime fiction: an exotic location for its international readers, hair-raising suspenseful sequences, perplexing puzzles, and sufficient violence and sex to keep things interesting. Yet hundreds of books of crime and mystery fiction are published every year with these same elements. The key to the success of Stieg Larsson's trilogy can be summed up in two words: Lisbeth Salander.

In the popular feminist magazine *Bust*, Salander is touted as a role model, a "subversive hacker, ass-kicking feminist, and vengeful genius."[1] Salander projects counterculture coolness; she has been damaged but takes brutal revenge on those who have hurt her. She is also a savant: a brilliant hacker and private investigator with a photographic memory. She is the ultimate rebel, who is entirely self-contained and does not need to depend on anyone else. Salander has been described as "a contemporary feminist heroine . . . [a] tech-savvy, take-no-crap goth bisexual."[2] True/Slant calls her a "tiny terminator."[3] And feminist activist Laurie Penny wrote,

> Lisbeth Salander is an immensely powerful character, a misandrist vigilante with a penchant for black fetish wear and ersatz technology, like the terrifying offspring of Batman and Valerie Solanos. . . . Salander is smart, she's brave, she always wins, and she won't let anyone tell her what to do. No wonder so many women secretly want to be her.[4]

Larsson's companion Eve Gabrielsson has reported that Larsson wrote the books to protest violence against women (the original Swedish title of the trilogy, *Men Who Hate Women*, was rejected by the English-language publishers as "too confrontational"). As Penny wrote, "Larsson . . . was disgusted by sexual violence, having witnessed the gang rape of a young girl when he was fifteen. According to a friend of his, the author never forgave himself for failing to help the girl, whose name was Lisbeth—just like the young heroine of the trilogy, who is also a rape survivor."[5] The section headings of the first book of the trilogy all provide statistics about violence against women: for example, "Forty-six percent of the women in Sweden have been subjected to violence by a man," and, "Thirteen percent of the women in Sweden have been subjected to aggravated sexual assault outside of a sexual relationship."[6]

So, what's the problem? I would be the last person to criticize Larsson for wanting to draw the public's attention to the very real abuses perpetrated against women, and I sincerely hope that the enormous popularity of his books has helped raise public consciousness about violence against women. Still, I fear that however noble Larsson's aim, his effect is potentially harmful. Although Lisbeth's "cool" factor is beyond dispute, she has been deliberately "styled" in a manner designed to titillate the reader. On the surface, Salander may seem like a "riot grrrl" for the twenty-first century, but at a deeper level, her character is presented as a sexual spectacle for the reader's voyeuristic pleasure.

Escapism or Exposure?

Crime and mystery fiction functions as escapism. Readers vicariously experience the excitement of dangerous and bloody murders as they solve the mystery along with the main characters. I have no complaint with reading to escape; otherwise, so much fiction (including the entire horror, sci-fi, and fantasy genres) would be replaced with the most naturalistic, gruelingly realistic texts.

In the case of *The Girl with the Dragon Tattoo*, however, the reader moves beyond escapism and into the role of perverse voyeur or "Peeping Tom." In her essay "Visual Pleasure and Narrative Cinema," Laura Mulvey wrote that in cinema,

> [The] male gaze projects its fantasy onto the female figure, which is styled accordingly. In the traditional exhibitionist role women are simultaneously looked at and displayed, with their appearance coded for strong visual and erotic impact. . . . Women displayed as sexual object is the *leitmotif* of sexual spectacle.[7]

These remarks also apply to the reader of the printed text who, as she reads, is projecting his/her own fantasies on Lisbeth Salander. Because it is hard to empathize with Salander, readers, male and female both, are less likely to see themselves reflected in her and therefore more likely to fantasize about her as an outside object. Consider the first description of Salander in *The Girl with the Dragon Tattoo*:

> [Salander] was a pale, anorexic young woman who had hair as short as a fuse, and a pierced nose and eyebrows. She had a wasp tattoo about an inch long on her neck, a tattooed loop around the biceps of her left arm and another around her left ankle . . . she had a dragon

tattoo on her left shoulder blade . . . she dyed her hair raven black. She looked as though she had just escaped from a week-long orgy with a gang of hard rockers. . . . She had simply been born thin, with slender bones that made her look girlish and fine-limbed with small hands, narrow wrists, and childlike breasts. She was twenty-four, but she sometimes looked fourteen.[8]

Later the reader also learns that she is "four feet eleven and weighed ninety pounds."[9] Female readers are unlikely to resemble or realistically covet Salander's extreme physical appearance; in fact, were she one inch shorter, she could medically be termed a "dwarf" or a "little person."

Larsson presents Salander's sexual identity and encounters in a manner that makes her a sexual object. Her experiences are a titillating sexual spectacle for the male reader, instead of just a caution against rape and sexual abuse. She becomes the equivalent of torture porn for men who read the trilogy and the object for their sexual fantasies.[10] Blomkvist, Berger, and Salander all have active sex lives, but the most explicit sex scenes in the books are those in which Lisbeth is being abused or exploited. Some readers might view this as a "cautionary tale"; readers are supposed to recoil from these scenes as they find themselves face-to-face with the explicit reality of sexual violence against women. Yet it seems there is another dimension present. As Penny wrote,

> It is clear that the author of the Millennium franchise did not intend to glamorize violence against women. Unfortunately, it's rather hard to stop the heart racing when rapes and murders are taking place in gorgeous high-definition over a slick soundtrack . . . Decorating a punchy pseudo-feminist revenge fantasy in the gaudy packaging of crime drama rather muddles Larsson's message. "Misogynist violence is appalling," the series seems to whisper; "now here's some more."[11]

Taraneh Ghajar Jerven agrees, saying, "Larsson's vivid scenes of sexual violence against women, particularly Salander, occur so frequently that it's hard not to question whether they're there as much for titillation as social commentary."[12] She notes the proliferation of such instances of violence in the books, saying they "brim with scenes where women are set on fire, beheaded, and choked with sanitary napkins . . . one girl is raped by both her father and her brother; prostitutes are carelessly killed."[13] There is also an uncomfortable element of pedophilia present in the abuse scenes involving Salander; she is frequently described as appearing physically adolescent, and "All the Evil" began when she was not yet thirteen. Anna Westerståhl Stenport and Cecilia Ovesdotter Alm note, "In terms of sexuality, Salander is a popular culture fantasy—adolescent-looking yet sexually experienced."[14]

Most of the consensual sexual encounters in the trilogy take place "off-screen"—the reader is made aware of them, but Larsson does not describe them in full detail. That is not the case, however, with the scenes of sexual violence. For example, when Salander's new unscrupulous and perverted guardian Bjurman coerces her into oral sex, every aspect of the encounter is graphically presented to the reader, from the smell of Bjurman's genitals to the duration and mechanics of the act itself. When Salander sets a trap for Bjurman in order to blackmail him and negate his legal hold on her money and actions, she miscalculates his level of sadism as he chains her to the bed and anally rapes her, which Larsson once again describes in detail.

Salander's lover Miriam Wu is associated with the BDSM community (a fact of which the reader is repeatedly reminded), and at one point in *The Girl Who Played with Fire*, Salander and Wu engage in sexual role-playing. Wu tells Salander, "Tonight I think I'll be a dominating bitch. I get to make the decisions."[15] She orders Salander to take off her clothes and lie on the floor, and binds her arms and blindfolds her. Salander even thinks, "This was similar to the way Nils Fucking Slimebag Bjurman had tied her up two years ago."[16] Yet it is also the only time in the trilogy that Salander is described as being sexually aroused. "Salander felt only lustful anticipation. . . . She was more excited than she had been in a long time."[17] Moreover, the sex act is described in greater detail than any other previous same-sex encounter: "She felt Mimmi's tongue on her belly and her fingers on the insides of her thighs."[18] Larsson is linking sexual violence and eroticism and also providing opportunities for the "male gaze" of the reader's voyeurism.

As Jerven says, "no female abuse scene was too explicit" for Larsson.[19] During Salander's rape, the reader is "treated" to a description of "the excruciating pain as [Bjurman] forced something up [Salander's] anus," as well as the fact that she "spent the week in bed with pain in her abdomen, bleeding from her rectum."[20] As Jerven notes, "[the] defense of this holds that depicting violence against women is okay because by showing it, he's commenting on how widespread/problematic it is."[21] Yet that seems like a bit of a slick explanation when one considers the proliferation of such instances in the trilogy.

In the third book, Larsson provides even *more* details of the rape. Blomkvist has encouraged Salander to create a written record of the abuse she suffered as part of her defense during her murder trial, in which she "identified the implements he had used during the rape, which included a short whip, an anal plug, a rough dildo, and clamps, which he attached to her nipples."[22] Salander wrote, "He asked if I liked being pierced and then left the room. He came back with a needle, which he pushed through my right nipple."[23] Salander also discusses "All the Evil" that has shaped her life; in the mental hospital she was "strapped . . . to a steel-framed bed for more than a year," force-fed psychotropic drugs, and repeatedly placed in sensory deprivation conditions.[24] The entire account of the trial reads as a grueling play-by-play of the enormous and seemingly never-ending abuses Salander has suffered.

The Desensitized Audience

By the end of the trilogy, the reader may be jaded and desensitized to these violent accounts. Personally, when I reached the description of "All the Evil" in the second book, I was surprised that it was not *worse!* As Gail Dines wrote, "Rather than being defined as 'deviant,' men's violence against women was analyzed and understood as *predictable* in a women-hating culture."[25] Although Salander never blames herself for the rape, she, too, sees it as predictable. Larsson wrote, "By the time she was eighteen, Salander did not know a single girl who at some point had not been forced to perform some sort of sexual act against her will . . . in her world, this was the natural order of things. As a girl she was legal prey."[26] This does not stop Salander from taking revenge on her attacker, but it also demonstrates an outlook central to the novels: such assaults are inevitable, unavoidable, and to be expected. Salander's response, "There's no point whimpering about it," shows it is the immutable status quo.[27] Stenport and Alm agree:

> The fact that Salander is instrumental in covering up all crimes of sexual violence committed against women in the [first] novel, including those so savagely directed at herself, cements a world order in which the notion of feminist solidarity and gender-neutral social regulation is completely erased.[28]

The Swedish film versions were rated R, so the viewer could expect that the sexual violence in the books would be slightly minimized. The rape scenes, though, are still graphically portrayed and visually disturbing. Yet there is a shift in focus. The anal rape takes place without any of the additional tortures and devices Salander describes in the books. Moreover, the scene in which Salander takes revenge on Bjurman is significantly longer and more explicit than the rape scenes. On camera, she sodomizes him with a dildo and kicks him repeatedly.

The camera also lingers on the image of his battered, bleeding, crudely tattooed chest. In the books, the reader's vision is primarily focused on the violence against Salander; in the film, the viewer's gaze is focused on the revenge Salander takes for that violence.

In the first film, Salander is also more directly complicit in the death of Martin Vanger. Larsson's version has her driving away after seeing his car catch fire. In the Swedish film, she forces him off the road and stands staring at him while he burns to death, refusing to act as he pleads for help. When reporting his death to Blomkvist, Salander admits that she could have saved him but says he deserved to die. On one level, these plot changes can be seen as empowering Salander beyond her role in the novel, but there is also another possible explanation; socially, violence against women is considered less acceptable than violence against men.

Salander's bisexuality is also much less overt in the films; there is a single scene of her waking naked next to another woman, whom the viewer may presume to be Wu but who never reappears. In contrast, the sex scene between Salander and Blomkvist is fairly lengthy and explicit, and the film's ending leaves room for a continuation of their romantic relationship. Thus, the changes in the films may serve to make them more "acceptable" to the audience.

Lisbeth Salander: A Complex Heroine

ABC News reported a reassuring fact regarding *The Girl with the Dragon Tattoo*:

> Music Box Films, US distributors for "The Girl with the Dragon Tattoo," are sending the Swedish movie to rape crisis centers and college groups who will show it to support victims of sexual assault.
>
> So far 125 have signed up, and they are prepared to give away thousands of DVD's for free.

The company has partnered with the Rape, Abuse, and Incest National Network (RAINN) to use the films as part of an educational program to advocate for trauma victims and bring attention to assault prevention.[29]

The article also reports that Amanda Sandberg, a twenty-four-year-old survivor of a violent rape, responded to the novels and the first film by saying, "It was very cathartic reading the books, and when I watched the first movie I was blown away. . . . It was the first active and aggressive depiction of a survivor that I have ever seen." Although the subtexts of the books may be complicated and somewhat contradictory, the story is at least partly functioning on a social level the way Larsson intended.

Although I truly am a fan of the books and of Lisbeth Salander, I believe that we should more fully investigate the subtext in the novels and the complexities of Salander's character, rather than blindly embracing her as a feminist role model. While the novels and the films, on one level, expose and condemn sexual violence against women and celebrate Salander's refusal to accept victim status, they also appeal to the readers'/viewers' prurient curiosity and voyeuristic urges by turning Salander into a sexual spectacle. As Dines wrote, "No woman was put on this earth to be hurt or humiliated in order to facilitate male masturbation."[30] We might consider to what extent we are complicit in women's abuse while we continue to enjoy and learn from Larsson's story.

NOTES

1. "The Girl Who Kicked the Hornet's Nest (review)," *Bust*, 2010, p. 54.

2. Taraneh Ghajar Jerven, "The Girl Who Doubted Stieg Larsson's Feminism," *Bitch Magazine: Feminist Response to Pop Culture*, no. 48, 2010, p. 9.

3. Susan Toepfer, "'Girl with the Dragon Tattoo': Lisbeth Salander Makes My Day," at http://trueslant.com/susantoepfer/2010/05/24/girl-with-the-dragon-tattoo-lisbeth-salander-makes-my-day/.

4. Laurie Penny, "Girls, Tattoos and Men Who Hate Women," *New Statesman*, www.newstatesman.com/blogs/laurie-penny/2010/09/women-girl-real-violence.

5. Ibid.

6. Stieg Larsson, *The Girl with the Dragon Tattoo*, trans. Reg Keeland (New York: Vintage, 2009), p. 127; ibid., p. 273.

7. Laura Mulvey, "Visual Pleasure and Narrative Cinema," in Vincent B. Leitch, ed., *The Norton Anthology of Theory and Criticism* (New York: W. W. Norton, 2001), pp. 2, 186.

8. Larsson, *The Girl with the Dragon Tattoo*, p. 38.

9. Ibid., p. 113.

10. *Torture porn* is a term sometimes used to describe films and other media works that graphically depict extreme violence, sometimes coupled with graphic sexual situations. In the many of the works of the genre, the violence is specifically directed against women. One oft-quoted example of the genre is Gaspar Noe's film *Irreversible*, which includes a nine-minute-long scene of a pregnant woman being anally raped. Torture porn also may be linked to more extreme genres such as snuff films, which depict death or murder. The actual existence of snuff films is debatable; many so-called snuff films such as *Cannibal Holocaust* were actually filmed using special effects, and others have been exposed as mere urban legends. Yet torture porn and related genres present a fetishized depiction of violence that may be presumed to be simultaneously repellent and seductive to the consumer.

11. Penny, "Girls, Tattoos and Men Who Hate Women."

12. Jerven, "The Girl Who Doubted Stieg Larsson's Feminism," p. 9.

13. Ibid.

14. Anna Westerståhl Stenport and Cecilia Ovesdotter Alm, "Corporations, Crime, and Gender Construction in Stieg Larsson's *The Girl with the Dragon Tattoo*," *Scandinavian Studies* 81, no. 2 (2009): 168.

15. Stieg Larsson, *The Girl Who Played with Fire*, trans. Reg Keeland (New York: Vintage, 2010), p. 138.

16. Ibid.

17. Ibid.

18. Ibid.

19. Jerven, "The Girl Who Doubted Stieg Larsson's Feminism," p. 9.

20. Larsson, *The Girl with the Dragon Tattoo*, p. 250; ibid., p. 252.

21. Jerven, "The Girl Who Doubted Stieg Larsson's Feminism," p. 9.

22. Stieg Larsson, *The Girl Who Kicked the Hornet's Nest*, trans. Reg Keeland (New York: Alfred A. Knopf, 2010), p. 319.

23. Ibid., p. 320.

24. Ibid., p. 487.

25. Gail Dines, "From Fantasy to Reality: Unmasking the Pornography Industry," in Robin Morgan, ed., *Sisterhood Is Forever: The Women's Anthology for a New Millennium* (New York: Washington Square Press, 2003), p. 306.

26. Larsson, *The Girl with the Dragon Tattoo*, p. 228.

27. Ibid.

28. Stenport and Alm, "Corporations, Crime, and Gender Construction in Stieg Larsson's *The Girl with the Dragon Tattoo*," pp. 170–171.

29. Susan Donaldson James, "Rape Victims Applaud Power of Stieg Larsson Films to Educate," http://abcnews.go.com/Health/MindMoodResourceCenter/stieg-larssons-film-girl-dragon-tattoo-teaches-college/story?id=11490699.

30. Dines, "From Fantasy to Reality: Unmasking the Pornography Industry," p. 314.

PART FOUR

"EVERYONE HAS SECRETS"

How can a man conceal his character?
—Confucius

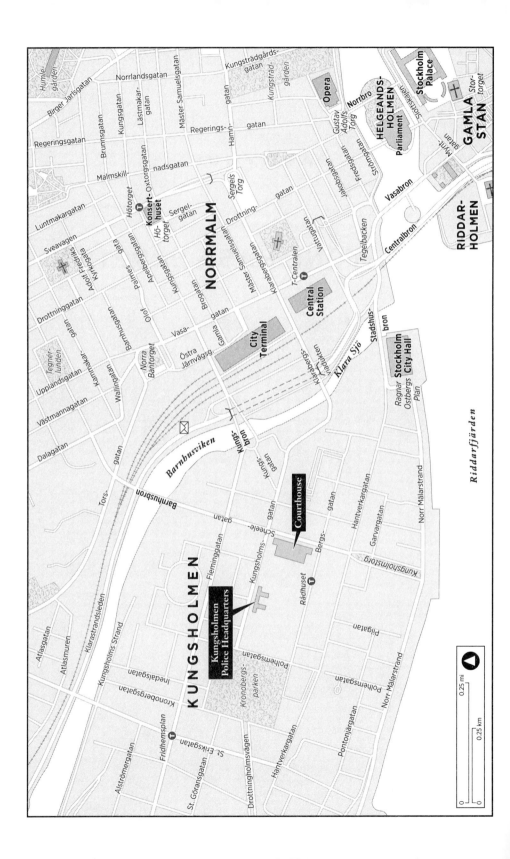

HACKER'S REPUBLIC: INFORMATION JUNKIES IN A FREE SOCIETY

Andrew Zimmerman Jones

In July 2010, an enigmatic figure took the stage at the TEDGlobal conference in Oxford. Identified by various sources as either a criminal or an activist, a hacker or a journalist, a digital terrorist or a humanitarian, Julian Assange is the cofounder and the public face of Wikileaks. An informal poll of the TEDGlobal audience showed that far more attendees felt that he was a "people's hero" than a "dangerous troublemaker."[1] (The possibility that he, like Lisbeth, might simultaneously be both was not raised.)

Wikileaks proclaims, "We help you safely get the truth out. We are of assistance to peoples of all countries who wish to reveal unethical behavior in their governments and institutions. We aim for maximum political impact."[2]

Here's how it works. A person has his or her hands on damaging videos or documents, which the individual feels should be exposed. Anonymously, the person gives the videos or the documents to Wikileaks, which then vets the materials for authenticity and coordinates their release.

Since its founding in 2006, Wikileaks has disseminated information as diverse as the "Climategate" e-mails, secret Scientology manuals, and evidence of African government corruption. In 2010 alone, Wikileaks released video footage of U.S. soldiers attacking a group of mostly unarmed citizens in Baghdad, a compilation of more than 76,900 documents about the war in Afghanistan, and the "Iraq War Logs" (consisting of more than 400,000 documents). Perhaps most infamously, Wikileaks began to release more than 250,000 U.S. diplomatic cables. All told, Wikileaks has a résumé of social impact that would certainly make the staff of *Millennium* sit up and take notice.

Assange's controversy began at a young age when "as a teenager he became Australia's most famous ethical computer hacker."[3] Following some of Wikileaks' biggest successes, Assange has become the epicenter of an international criminal investigation, accused (to varying degrees) of theft, espionage, aiding terrorists, and sexual assault. He has responded by calling it a smear campaign conducted by governments he has exposed. Sound familiar? Commentators have said that Wikileaks "is a story as intriguing and confusing as a Stieg Larsson blockbuster" and it "has more twists, turns and conspiracy theories than any of Stieg Larsson's best-sellers."[4] The editor in chief of the *New York Times* called the introduction to an e-book detailing the *Times*'s interactions with Wikileaks and Assange "The Boy Who Kicked the Hornet's Nest."[5]

What Is a Hacker?

Lisbeth Salander is not a famous hacker like Julian Assange, but she takes pride in being one of the best. The hacker culture is the only one that she fully embraces. It isn't something she dabbles in, like her connection with the Evil Fingers rock band. Yet even though hacking is a central component of her character, Lisbeth hides it from everyone except the Hacker Republic and Blomkvist. Given the reputation of hackers, it's not hard to understand why.

Assange himself is not so quick to accept the hacker label these days. When asked about his hacking background at TEDGlobal, Assange replied, "Well, I was a journalist. . . . I was a very young journalist activist. . . . I wrote a magazine, was prosecuted for it when I was a teenager. So you have to be careful with *hacker*. . . . There's a method that can be deployed for various things. Unfortunately, at the moment, it's being deployed by the Russian mafia in order to steal your grandmother's bank accounts. So this phrase is not as nice as it used to be."[6]

Most people use the term *hacker* to mean someone who breaks into a computer system in order to gain access to private information, which is the same way that Assange, Larsson, and Salander seem to apply the term. Not everyone agrees, though. The hacker community tends to view hacking as a creative effort to overcome problems, both inside and outside of the computing realm. An online database of hacker terminology, the *Jargon File*, applies an entirely different term, *cracker*, to those who use their skills destructively: to break security, create computer viruses, or otherwise damage computer systems.[7]

Swedish communications professor Jonas Löwgren (it's best to get the Swedes involved early) has identified three distinct forms of hacking, based largely on their origins: hobby hacking, academic hacking, and network hacking.[8] hobby hackers started in their garages with ham radio kits; the academic hackers started at MIT with model trains; and the network hackers started by tricking telephone systems into giving free long distance.[9] All three paths eventually led to the computer.

For these early hackers, "a project undertaken or a product built not solely to fulfill some constructive goal, but with some wild pleasure taken in mere involvement, was called a 'hack.'"[10] The academic hacker, like the hobby hacker, was motivated by the sheer enthusiasm of pushing the system's limits but usually published an academic paper along the way.

Although the concept of hacking came of age around electronics and computing, it is now regularly applied outside of these areas. According to Burrell Smith, the creator of the Macintosh computer, "Hackers can do almost anything. . . . You can be a hacker carpenter. . . . I think it has to do with craftsmanship and caring about what you're doing."[11] (The original use of the term *hacker* was "someone who makes furniture with an axe," so in a sense the phrase "hacker carpenter" could be seen as redundant.)[12]

Hackers themselves have defined the term in a number of different ways (eight ways to be precise), which range from narrow to broad in scope, including

- "One who programs enthusiastically (even obsessively) or who enjoys programming rather than just theorizing about programming."
- "An expert at a particular program, or one who frequently does work using it or on it."
- "An expert or enthusiast of any kind."
- "One who enjoys the intellectual challenge of creatively overcoming or circumventing limitations."
- "A malicious meddler who tries to discover sensitive information by poking around."[13]

When Benjamin Franklin crafted the first bifocal lens, he was hacking eyeglasses. In fact, the entire scientific enterprise can be seen as trying to hack nature. McKenzie Wark implies this when he describes "the hacker class, which finds new ways of making nature productive, which discovers new patterns in the data thrown off by nature."[14]

It is becoming more mainstream to think of science as a hacker enterprise. Genetic manipulation is called "hacking the genome." A recent book titled *Hack the Planet* describes technology's potential to remedy climate issues before they are irreparable, while *Astronomy Hacks: Tips and Tools for Observing the Night Sky* is a popular introductory book for budding star-gazers.

The Hacker Ethic

In 1984, Stephen Levy was one of the first journalists to outline a "hacker ethic."[15]

- Access to computers—and anything that might teach you something about the way the world works—should be unlimited and total. Always yield to the Hands-On Imperative!
- All information should be free.
- Mistrust authority—promote decentralization.
- Hackers should be judged by their hacking, not by bogus criteria such as degrees, age, race, or position.
- You can create art and beauty on a computer.
- Computers can change your life for the better.

In this short list, we begin to see some of the reasons why this culture appeals to Lisbeth. The hacker culture is neither good nor evil but instead focuses on getting results. It is self-reliant and rooted in an antiauthoritarian embrace of individuality. No citizen is beholden to any single person, only to the quality of work being done.

By the mid-1990s, it became clear that computers were not a peripheral form of technology, accessible only to the nerdy elite in their garages, but were becoming central to the way individuals ran their lives, industries ran their businesses, and governments ran their bureaucracies. The potentially destructive power of hacking was clear. In 1997, an anthropology professor (cyberanthropology, in fact) analyzed hacker texts and proposed a new set of ethics for the 1990s hacker.[16] The new ethic included a concern over abuse, with new ethical concerns that focused on privacy and social responsibility.

Lisbeth alludes to this stronger sense of social responsibility when she says, "I also have principles. . . . I call them *Salander's Principles*. One of them is that a bastard is always a bastard, and if I can hurt a bastard by digging up shit about him, then he deserves it."[17] Assange identifies similar motivations when describing the values at the core of his own work. "Capable, generous men do not create victims; they nurture victims."[18] This is a statement that could have been made of Blomkvist, Palmgren, or Armansky.

Though Lisbeth has no problem busting heads in real life, her hacking emphasizes stealth. She may implant secret programs that create mirror networks over the Internet, but she doesn't create viruses for the sake of generating mayhem. "Her trespassing in [Armansky's] computer was not malicious: she just wanted to know what the company was working on, to see the lay of the land."[19]

Assange also values stealth, as outlined in guidelines offered in a 1997 book: "don't damage computer systems you break into (including crashing them); don't change the information in those systems (except for altering logs to cover your tracks); and share information."[20] Lisbeth seems to live by these rules as well.

In yet another analysis, the hacker ethic is exemplified by a set of core values. Hackers meld *passion* with *freedom*, creating *social worth* with *openness* (resulting in recognition), and an emphasis on *activity* toward a goal of *caring*.[21] A hacker who lives according to these principles is able to achieve the goal of all true hackers: a lifestyle based in *creativity*.

Lisbeth certainly succeeds on this score, though it seems to come as a surprise even to herself when she admits enjoying the recognition of her excellence:

[Blomkvist] had suddenly asked her if she was a good hacker.

To her own surprise she replied, "I'm probably the best in Sweden. There may be two or three others at about my level."

She did not doubt the accuracy of her reply. Plague had once been better than she was, but she had passed him long ago.

On the other hand, it felt funny to say the words. She had never done it before. She had never had an outsider to have this sort of conversation with, and she enjoyed the fact that he seemed impressed by her talents.[22]

The relationship between Blomkvist and Salander is based largely on the synergy of their ethical goals. Blomkvist devotes his life as a journalist to uncovering information and making it available to the public, in the belief that "information should be free." Lisbeth, on the other hand, is locked in survival mode. Her hacking is motivated primarily by her self-interest and also by the recognition she receives from her peers: Plague, Trinity, and the other members of Hacker Republic. This changes when Blomkvist gives her the opportunity to expose Wennerström. Though her personal role is not known to many, the positive outcome is a clear vindication of her talents by the world at large.

It's no wonder that Salander and Blomkvist bond. He takes the work at the core of her being, her hacking, and gives it a deeper meaning.

The Hacker Millennium

Many young people today do not think about ownership the same way that their parents did. The digital revolution and the mainstreaming of hacker culture have resulted in a world where boundaries of ownership are rapidly changing.

The tech-savvy youth of today download music and stream videos, never holding anything as prosaic as a CD or a DVD in their hands. These new methods create all kinds of questions of ownership, including how to appropriately apply copyright protections in the digital age. Salander is described as "an information junkie with a delinquent child's take on morals and ethics."[23] A publisher, a producer, an artist, or an author might similarly describe someone like this who downloads his or her copyrighted work from the Internet for free (or Julian Assange, for that matter).

This transformation in the way we view intellectual property is straight out of the hacker ethic. "Stealing . . . from a large institution like a corporation or government is OK. Stealing . . . from an individual or small nonprofit is not. . . . Thus the new hacker ethic . . . does not embrace theft; instead it simply defines certain things (like information) as not being personal property, or certain actions (using phone service) as 'borrowing' rather than theft."[24]

This belief in free information also has positive manifestations. The most potent single source of information ever created is Wikipedia, the volunteer-written encyclopedia that is accessible, for free, to anyone in the world, with articles that cover virtually any topic imaginable. Wikipedia is the ultimate manifestation of the idea that "Information wants to be free but is everywhere in chains."[25]

Lisbeth clearly feels comfortable gaining access to information she wants at any time, prompting Blomkvist to say, "We need to have a talk on the subject of what's yours and what's mine."[26] Everyone wants his or her own information to be secure, of course. Lisbeth goes to great lengths to maintain her personal privacy, without considering anyone else's. And, of course, Wikileaks could not function without the fog of anonymity it creates around whistleblowers.

The Mighty Citizen

Individuals want privacy, businesses want privacy, and governments want privacy. In his nonfiction book *The Transparent Society*, science fiction author David Brin explores the issue by distinguishing between privacy for individual citizens and privacy for "the mighty," which includes both corporations and governments. So, where does one draw the line between the citizen and the mighty in *The Millennium Trilogy*?

At the end of *The Girl with the Dragon Tattoo*, Blomkvist agrees to suppress the truth about Martin Vanger. Is this act in the interest of the personal privacy of Harriet Vanger or the mighty interest of the Vanger Corporation? In this case, the secrecy serves both interests. It is Salander who lays things bare for Blomkvist: "which is worse—the fact that Martin Vanger raped her out in the cabin or that you're going to do it in print?"[27] Moments later, she extorts the Vanger Corporation to provide some form of social justice, in the form of money, for Martin's many victims and also for other abuse victims.

The situation is not nearly so easy for Blomkvist, because it straddles the two realms: the personal and the mighty. His ethical considerations include the belief that "Bastards too have a right to their private lives."[28] Yet he also believes in reporting the truth, and a crime had been committed that was worth reporting. "He who had lambasted his colleagues for not publishing the truth, here he sat, discussing, negotiating even, the most macabre cover-up he had ever heard of."[29]

Though Blomkvist consents to the cover-up, it is clear that he still has reservations, and as a journalist, Larsson himself may have experienced some cognitive dissonance over Blomkvist's decision. Indeed, this might be why he has Henrik Vanger offer Blomkvist's defense:

> You had to choose between your role as a journalist and your role as a human being. I could never have bought your silence. And I'm quite certain that you would have exposed us if Harriet had turned out in some way to have been implicated, or if you thought I was a cretin.[30]

Salander, however, never had to make that choice. As a hacker, she followed her own set of principles and was able to hack a course of moral certainty out of the path that, for journalist Blomkvist, led to an ethical dilemma.

Watching the Watchers

David Brin begins his analysis of privacy with a description of two high-tech cities of the future that are free of crime, thanks to the ubiquitous placement of surveillance cameras. In one, the cameras report to a central Police Department, where the government maintains strict regulations on its citizens. In the other, any citizen may gain access to any camera at any time. The technology is here, so the question he asks is, "Who will ultimately control the cameras?"[31] Will it be the mighty or the citizens?

Brin argues in favor of putting the access and the authority in the hands of the citizens to enforce accountability. If we try to keep it from individuals, then the corporations and the governments (having more resources) will still find a way to get it. So it will be the individuals who lose out on their privacy. His conclusion is based on reasoning somewhat similar to the 2010 Supreme Court verdict in *Citizens United v. Federal Election Commission*: If we give the access and the authority to the individual, the corporations (and the government) will have it by default as entities composed of individuals. No one loses out, and most people gain.

Brin outlines a decentralized, transparent, Wikileaks-like approach to creating accountability. Eight years after Brin's book was published, Wikileaks was founded, throwing light into the dark corners of Brin's "mighty," while, at the same time, protecting the secrecy of their own sources, whom Assange describes as "classical whistleblowers." In Assange's words, "Very rarely do we ever know [the source's identity]. And if we find out at some stage then we destroy that information as soon as possible."[32]

This reflects the conflicting values in the hacker ethic (and Brin's *Transparent Society*): personal privacy coupled with widespread openness in areas of public interest. "[T]here's enormous pressures [*sic*] to harmonize freedom of speech legislation and transparency legislation around the world. . . . That's why it's a very interesting time to be in, because with just a little bit of effort, we can shift it one way or another."[33]

Assange is proud of his accomplishments, proclaiming his prowess as unabashedly as Lisbeth does. In response to growing concern over the number of classified documents Wikileaks releases, Assange replied, "It's a worry—isn't it?— that the rest of the world's media is doing such a bad job that a little group of activists is able to release more of that type of information than the rest of the world press combined."[34]

Those who believe that Assange is moral might well think of him, as Palmgren did of Salander, that his "notion of morality did not always coincide with that of the justice system."[35] And, certainly, the justice system has taken notice of Assange.

The Hornet's Nest

The United States is uncertain how (or whether) to charge Assange for the theft of classified government documents. The army private believed to be responsible, Bradley Manning, is being held in military detention, but it's not clear whether Assange or Wikileaks actually violated any laws. Assange claims that he had no contact with Manning and in fact never heard the name until word of his arrest hit the media, which matches his description of how Wikileaks works with sources. The government can't pin any conspiracy charges on Assange without establishing that he collaborated with Manning, encouraging him to steal the documents.

In *The Girl with the Dragon Tattoo*, Blomkvist collaborates with Lisbeth, encouraging her to steal the Wennerström information. Though he treats her as a source, he's skirting an ethical line there, one that Assange has structured Wikileaks to avoid. This doesn't necessarily protect Assange or Wikileaks from arrest. Journalists hold certain legal protections when acquiring information, but Assange's status as a journalist—despite his self-identification—is less than clear. The *New York Times*, at least, "regarded Assange throughout as a source, not as a partner or collaborator."[36]

Certainly, Assange is a self-identified activist, rather than a dispassionate, objective reporter of events. Wikileaks released the full, unedited footage of the Baghdad helicopter attack but also packaged it as a short antiwar propaganda film titled "Collateral Murder" . . . an adaptation of events that "didn't call attention to an Iraqi who was toting a rocket-propelled grenade."[37]

In addition, Assange is fighting charges of sexual assault (in Sweden, of all places). The details of the allegations are hidden behind lawyers and Swedish privacy laws. Under the most generous interpretation, Assange has seemingly been revealed to the world as someone who treats women (at least, those he sleeps with) appallingly, which puts his "people's hero" title in question.

It is unclear whether Assange will be found guilty of sexual crimes in Sweden or espionage crimes in the United States, but clearly the role and the rights of transparency in our information society will be put to the legal test. Even without official legal action, Wikileaks servers have been voluntarily dropped by their host, Amazon.com, forcing Wikileaks to relocate to European servers. In addition, PayPal has suspended the account where Wikileaks collected donations.

Hackers have been preparing for such a fight for years, and cyberattacks against Wikileaks' critics have been launched. John Perry Barlow, the cofounder of the digital-rights advocacy organization the Electronic Frontier Foundation, tweeted, "The first serious infowar is now engaged. The field of battle is Wikileaks. You are the troops."[38]

Of all of the labels given to Lisbeth Salander throughout *The Millennium Trilogy*, about the only one that she willingly accepts is "hacker." This is not a random choice or a mere plot convenience. The proper use of information and the damage caused by obscuring it are at the heart of the trilogy. By making his two primary characters a journalist and a hacker, Stieg Larsson has created a new kind of hero for our modern information age.

NOTES

1. TEDGlobal 2010 interview, "Julian Assange: Why the World Needs Wikileaks." Video and text available at www.ted.com/.

2. Wikileaks mirror homepage, http://mirror.wikileaks.info/.

3. *Personal Democracy Forum*, PDF Conference 2010: Speakers.

4. Angella Johnson, "Supporters dismissed rape accusations against Wikileaks founder Julian Assange . . . but the two women involved tell a different story," *Daily Mail*, August 29, 2010; Dana Kennedy, "'Sex by Surprise' at Heart of Assange Criminal Probe," *AOL News*, December 2, 2010.

5. Alexander Star, "Open Secrets: Wikileaks, War and American Diplomacy," New York Times Company, January 2010.

6. TEDGlobal 2010 interview, ibid.

7. *Jargon File*, maintained by Eric Raymond. Glossary: cracker.

8. February 23, 2000, Jonas Löwgren's lecture notes, "Hacker culture(s)."

9. Stephen Levy, *Hackers: Heroes of the Computer Revolution* (Sebastopol, CA: O'Reilly Media, 2010), chapter 1.

10. Ibid., p. 10.

11. Ibid., p. 459.

12. *Jargon File*, Glossary: hacker.

13. Ibid.

14. McKenzie Wark, *A Hacker Manifesto* (Cambridge, MA: Harvard University Press, 2004), paragraph 042.

15. Levy, *Hackers: Heroes of the Computer Revolution*, pp. 27–38.

16. Steven Mizrach, "Is There a Hacker Ethic for 90s Hackers?" 1997, http://www2.fiu.edu/~mizrachs/hackethic.html.

17. Stieg Larsson, *The Girl with the Dragon Tattoo*, trans. Reg Keeland (New York: Vintage, 2009), p. 344.

18. TEDGlobal 2010 interview, ibid.

19. Larsson, *The Girl Who Played with Fire*, trans. Reg Keeland (New York: Vintage, 2010), p. 107.

20. Suelette Dreyfus, with Julian Assange, *Underground: Hacking, Madness and Obsession on the Electronic Frontier* (London: Mandarin Publishing, 1997/2001).

21. Pekka Himanem, *The Hacker Ethic and the Spirit of the Information Age* (New York: Random House, 2001), pp. 139–141.

22. Larsson, *The Girl with the Dragon Tattoo*, p. 395.

23. Ibid., p. 384.

24. Mizrach, "Is There a Hacker Ethic for 90s Hackers?"

25. Wark, *A Hacker Manifesto*, paragraph 126.

26. Larsson, *The Girl with the Dragon Tattoo*, p. 383.

27. Ibid., p. 514.

28. Ibid., p. 344.

29. Ibid., p. 514.

30. Ibid., p. 586.

31. David Brin, *The Transparent Society: Will Technology Force Us to Choose between Privacy and Freedom?* (Reading, MA: Perseus Books, 1998), p. 6.

32. TEDGlobal 2010 interview.

33. Ibid.

34. Ibid.

35. Larsson, *The Girl Who Played with Fire*, p. 150.

36. Bill Keller, "Dealing with Assange and the Wikileaks Secrets," *New York Times*, January 26, 2011.

37. Star, *Open Secrets*.

38. Raphael Satter and Peter Svensson, "Wikileaks Fights to Stay Online amid Attacks," Associated Press, December 3, 2010.

KICKING THE HORNET'S NEST: THE HIDDEN "SECTION" IN EVERY INSTITUTION

Adriel M. Trott

The general expectation is that Lisbeth Salander should have as much chance as the next person to be properly protected by the relevant agencies of the government. Stieg Larsson suggests that institutions such as the police force, the media, and the Swedish intelligence agency simply need to be rid of the chauvinistic and self-serving men who pollute them. The institutions on their own are not the problem. The problem is the bad eggs that turn them rotten. The problem is with Advokat Nils Erik Bjurman and not with the guardianship agency, with Dr. Teleborian and not with psychiatric institutions, with Hans Faste and not with the police, with Prosecutor Ekström and not with the justice system, and with Evert Gullberg and not with the secret police. Larsson even has Blomkvist say,

> I don't believe in collective guilt. It concerns only those directly involved. The same is true of Säpo. I don't doubt

155

that there are excellent people working in Säpo. This is about a small group of conspirators.[1]

The notion that there is not collective guilt suggests that the problem is not inherent in institutions but is the responsibility of the individuals who make up the institutions. For example, Edklinth and Figuerola do not realize the institution has bias against women at its core and instead go to the prime minister to prompt an investigation to cleanse the Section of wrongdoers.

When the problem is how the law gets applied, however, it is no longer about individuals. Mia Johansson has just completed a dissertation, which alongside Dag Svensson's research will expose a number of high-powered johns who abuse women. Johansson's dissertation, *From Russia with Love*, reveals a madam who runs a brothel and is trafficking girls from Russia whom she turns into prostitutes by force. This madam is convicted of running a brothel but acquitted of the much worse crime of trafficking. The law cannot protect the girls who testify against the madam. The police cannot, or will not, find the girls. When asked about the tough laws Sweden has against trafficking and the sex trade, Svensson responds, "The law is pure window dressing."[2]

Svensson's response points to a deeper problem that has long troubled philosophers. If a law can be pure window dressing, perhaps there is something fundamentally wrong with the nature of the legal institution. Larsson's trilogy suggests that removing the few troublesome characters from these institutions is insufficient to address the underlying problem.

Just a Few Bad Apples or the Whole Darn Tree?

Institutions are organizations established by and for a community to institute the law. The word *institute* comes from the Latin word that means "to cause to stand." An institution helps the community to stand on its own, to be stable, to preserve itself as what it is over time. Jean-Jacques Rousseau (1712–1778) describes government as that which unites the will of the people to the power that puts that will to work.[3] The will of the people is expressed in the law, so institutions are organizations that give life to the law and create stability for the community. The police, the courts, psychiatric hospitals, secret police, the media, and even the family are all institutions meant to express the will of the people in *The Millennium Trilogy*.

Because institutions are what put the law to work, governmental institutions need to operate as the law does: neutrally and without passion. Aristotle (384–322 BCE) explains the position of those who support the rule of law over rule by men in this way: the law is reason without desire. Yet he goes on to explain that the law is made and applied by human beings so that even the law includes some element of human desire.[4] Like Aristotle, Larsson is suspicious of institutions championing neutrality, particularly because of their inherent need to preserve themselves. Rousseau explains that the government often becomes stronger than the will of the people because it is more concentrated.[5] He encourages vigilance to keep the government's power equal to the people's will. Because the government becomes stronger when it is more concentrated, the institutions that make up the government tend to have more power to preserve and protect themselves than the will of the people has to assert law.

Institutions, it appears, are incapable of the neutrality required for them to protect equally those who need the protection of the law. Consider, for example, Larsson's depiction of the Swedish intelligence agency, the Säkerhetspolisen, or Säpo, whose task was so-called personnel control. Säpo has been secretly taken over from within by "the Section," which claims to be "the last line of defense."[6] In its effort to protect Salander's father, Zalachenko, Säpo had Salander kept in a psychiatric institution when what she obviously needed was real guidance and support. The police not only failed to prosecute

Zalachenko for his crimes, including his savage assaults against Salander's mother, but the Section actively made the crimes go away. On top of all of that, it arranged for Salander to be under semipermanent guardianship by the state so that she did not even have control over her own finances. The institution acted nefariously just for the sake of protecting a man whose usefulness to the state did not seem to outlive his crimes. Säpo also set up a secret organization that was meant to protect the institution while operating outside of its purview.

This logic, whereby the institution preserves itself by acting illegally and then justifies this action by claiming self-defense, is an obvious problem for democratic communities. Democracies must assume the neutrality and the equality of institutions in order to have faith in the rule of law. Yet when institutions become biased in favor of themselves and their own existence, they invariably begin to subordinate the powerless, the very ones they are supposed to protect. By disseminating the idea that those who are subordinated or outright excluded (women, for example) are not worthy of protection, they justify their failure to protect them. Larsson shows how women are portrayed as unbalanced, irrational, abnormal, hysterical, sexually exploitable, all for the sake of men who maintain institutions. The dual role that institutions play in protecting women by subordination and stripping the same women of protections for the sake of the institution's own survival is manifest in the court's and the psychiatric hospital's treatment of Lisbeth. Similarly, the guardianship agency's desire to maintain guardianship of Salander shows us how the institution's self-preservation trumps the concern for the individual.

Even more appalling is the guardian agency's doublespeak regarding this tendency. Ulrika von Liebenstaahl from the agency says two things in court that are clearly shown to be false in Salander's case. First, she says, "There exists a rigorous supervision of guardianship cases."[7] If this were the case, then the agency would know about Bjurman's abuse and his sham reports. Then she says, "No-one is happier than we who work at the agency when a guardianship is rescinded."[8] If that were so, however, then the agency would be happiest to put itself out of business. Certainly, it doesn't appear to be in the nature of the institution to work toward such an end. The institution, as Rousseau tells us, becomes more powerful than the will of the people. So the institution's desire to maintain itself is at odds with its own mission, given by the law that it institutes.

Institutions cannot simply be swept clean of their corrupt elements; rather, they tend toward corruption in their very being. The injustice of the institution appears necessary for the very maintenance of the institution. The Section, for example, justifies its existence legally. A directive signed by Prime Minister Fälldin, which set aside funds for the "Section for Special Analysis," sanctioned a unit responsible for "internal personnel control" and could be understood as sanctioning the monitoring of sensitive individuals outside the Security Police, individuals such as the PM himself. So the PM legalizes activity that stands against the law and enables the institution to stand both inside and outside the law, at least in part for the sake of its own self-protection and stability.

Keeping Order versus Achieving Justice

Contemporary French philosopher Jacques Rancière distinguishes between the activity that preserves institutions, which he calls policing, and the activity that contests institutions, which he calls politics.[9] Policing should be distinguished from the work of men and women with badges and considered more broadly as administering the law. This administrating appears to be neutral and unbiased, but it is deceptively so. Its apparent neutrality is challenged by the political activity that disrupts policing. The effort to maintain institutions as they are resists the work of politics to question whether the institutions operate according to standards of equality.

When institutions close off the question of whether they are properly applying the law, they tend toward their own self-protection, which oftentimes requires the unequal application of the law and the refusal to recognize certain parties. Hannah Arendt (1906–1975) criticizes the ineffectual concept of "human rights" for just this reason when she explains that the problem with institutions is that their power is effective only insofar as they already recognize those with a claim to protection.[10] Those who are not recognized by the institution do not benefit from its protection. Arendt argues that it is precisely those people who need the help and support of the institution who are not recognized by the institution. Although the institution claims to be neutral, its lack of neutrality is evident in its failure to recognize equally all parties with claims to protection or support. Institutions see those whom they exclude, such as Salander, as necessarily not acceptable, not legitimate parties to any given dispute.

Salander herself challenges the notion that the institution can be redeemed by her recognition that it is pointless to speak with those in authority if they cannot hear the complaint. The institutions that she finds herself battling in her youth—the police, and behind them, Säpo and the psychiatric institution and its terrorizing leader, Dr. Teleborian—could not hear her because it was part of their task to show she was not worth listening to. Lisbeth was labeled insane by the very institutions that created a life for her in which she had to become someone who could defend herself with force. She did not defend herself to authority figures, and this refusal was taken as evidence that the authorities were justified in their treatment of her.

When Lisbeth tries to explain to Dr. Teleborian what she did to her father, who was specifically charged by Säpo to keep Salander committed, he responds thus, as she explains in court:

> He didn't want to listen to me. He claimed that I was fantasizing. And as punishment I was to be strapped

down until I stopped fantasizing. And then he tried to force-feed me psychotropic drugs.[11]

Salander's behavior was judged insane by those who created the standard of sanity in terms of what protects and supports the community. Yet those who resisted the community could not have a justifiable complaint against the system, because their behavior showed that they did not wish to support it. Consider how the court that is trying Salander cannot even see her lawyer's competence. Prosecutor Ekström challenges Giannini's capacity to defend Salander because she is a women's rights attorney, not a criminal attorney.

Lisbeth has believed that speaking to the authorities was useless because they could not hear her. So why suddenly in the courtroom does she think that she can or will be heard? Has the institution been properly cleaned up? Why should Salander think so? It's hard not to wonder whether Larsson is being overly optimistic here in a way that detracts from the critique that his trilogy offers. Why should the judge start to hear her, when no other authority that stood for the stability and the maintenance of order and the law has heard Salander? A story needs a good ending, and of course, it is satisfying to see Salander finally get to that warehouse and take care of business, but the question still stands. How can institutions be reformed if they tend toward corruption by virtue of what they are?

Institutions and Patriarchy: Men Who Hate Women

The idea that the structure of institutions and political life in general serves those in power comes from Karl Marx (1818–1883). Marx thought institutions served the rich, propertied class, but feminist thinkers have taken up Marx's analysis of political institutions to argue that institutions do indeed serve those in power, and men are those in power. In contrast to those who think that institutions can be constructed neutrally, as if we are all blind to our position in the world as John Rawls (1921–2002) argues, many feminist thinkers maintain that institutions are patriarchal both because they serve the interests of men and because they embody certain masculine traits.[12] bell hooks, for example, defines patriarchy in this way:

> Patriarchy is a political-social system that insists that males are inherently dominating, superior to everything and everyone deemed weak, especially females, and endowed with the right to dominate and rule over the weak and to maintain that dominance through various forms of psychological terrorism and violence.[13]

Throughout *The Millennium Trilogy*, it is difficult to ignore that this preservation of institutions at the expense of others' lives is largely perpetrated by men against women. Yet these institutions are also patriarchal because they champion the elements that we associate with masculinity and the authority of men. Institutions trumpet rationality, which comes to mean having no response to pleasure or pain. Salander and her femininity are a problem precisely because she actively responds to the emotional pain of seeing her father abuse her mother. Institutions boast stability, which means remaining the same in the face of abuse. So Salander needs the guardianship of the state because she resists and retaliates against sexual abuse. (There is a sense in the media and among the police that anyone who would tattoo what Salander did onto Bjurman must be a little off.) And institutions pronounce power, which suggests that you are subordinate because you can be subordinated. Hence, Salander should be under guardianship because she is under guardianship.

In each case, institutions rely on the apparent sanity and neutrality of institutions to accomplish their own extreme prejudice. For this reason, Blomkvist himself supports this patriarchy insofar as he does not think the institutions themselves, only their corrupt members, are the problem. ("I don't believe in collective guilt.") Lisbeth recognizes the problems of institutions themselves when she refuses to speak to the authorities, knowing that they have no reason to listen to her. In contrast to Mikael, who thinks that things can be made right, Lisbeth resists seeking institutional protection when the institutions doing the protection have proved themselves patriarchal. Lisbeth takes care of herself. Between her pepper spray, her Taser, and her quick thinking, she easily takes down two motorcycle gang members. Sure, she's small, but she's wily. We know she's smart. She's obviously tech-savvy. More than that, she thinks ahead, and she's tenacious. (It may also be true that Salander's independence is made possible because she came into a ton of money, which makes it clear that independence may be a matter not only of gender, but of how well-off someone is.) Notice how all of these things seem like clear signs of rationality—she tries to defend herself when attacked; she thinks through problems before they arise; she's capable of using the tools at her disposal in unique ways. Clearly, she does not need male protection, "guardianship," as the Swedish state makes it seem. Perhaps this is also why she resists Blomkvist's help. Yet when Lisbeth's strengths are put to use against the prevailing institutions, those institutions judge her insane to maintain their power.

Lisbeth's story depicts the high cost that patriarchal institutions exact from individuals who resist them. When a woman shows that she does not need or want men to administer her finances or her emotional life or to dictate her morals or to regulate her intellectual or social life, she displaces men from the place they took to be rightfully theirs. The focus of the whole *Millennium Trilogy* is on how Salander's father sought revenge against his daughter, as did Bjurman, and brought the force of the state and its powerful institutions to bear on this project. If we measure it by the response she gets, Salander is an obvious threat to her father's consequence-free existence. The passion and force with which the media and the Section slander Lisbeth show how vigorously institutions fight to preserve themselves. Yet Lisbeth shows again and again that she does not need their help. All the same, she does need institutions to be just in order to live her own life, free from harassment and abuse. But is that possible?

Rancière's distinction between "policing" and "politics" points to a solution. Policing is the effort to preserve institutions, and this effort tends to privilege the preservation of institutions over the responsibility of the institutions to those they serve. Politics puts into question the viability of the institution by questioning who is excluded from its protection. As *The Millennium Trilogy* makes clear, the solution cannot be to create new and better institutions that don't fall prey to this problem. Rather, the solution must be to encourage a politics that puts the power of institutions in question by continually disrupting and resisting their attempts to protect the status quo.[14]

NOTES

1. Stieg Larsson, *The Girl Who Kicked the Hornet's Nest*, trans. Reg Keeland (New York: Alfred A. Knopf, 2010), p. 212.

2. Stieg Larsson, *The Girl Who Played with Fire*, trans. Reg Keeland (New York: Vintage, 2010), p. 98.

3. Jean-Jacques Rousseau, "The Social Contract," in A. Ritter and J. C. Bondanella, eds., *Rousseau's Political Writings*, trans. J. C. Bondanella (New York: W. W. Norton, 1988), pp. 118–122.

4. Aristotle, *Politics*, III.15–16, trans. C. D. C. Reeve (Indianapolis: Hackett, 1998).

5. Rousseau, "The Social Contract," p. 121.

6. Larsson, *The Girl Who Kicked the Hornet's Nest*, p. 82.

7. Ibid., p. 470.

8. Ibid., p. 471.

9. Jacques Rancière, *Dis-Agreement: Politics and Philosophy*, trans. Julie Rose (Minneapolis: University of Minnesota, 1998), p. 28.

10. Hannah Arendt, "The Decline of the Nation-State and the End of the Rights of Man," in *Origins of Totalitarianism* (New York: Harcourt, Brace, Jovanovich, 1973), pp. 267–302.

11. Larsson, *The Girl Who Kicked the Hornet's Nest*, p. 490.

12. John Rawls, *A Theory of Justice* (Cambridge, MA: Harvard University Press, 1971). Also, see Carole Pateman, *The Sexual Contract* (Palo Alto, CA: Stanford University Press, 1988); Catherine MacKinnon, *Feminism Unmodified: Discourses on Life and Law* (Cambridge, MA: Harvard University Press, 1988).

13. bell hooks, *The Will to Change: Men, Masculinity and Love* (New York: Washington Square Press, 2004), p. 18.

14. I would like to thank Jill Gordon for recommending Larsson's trilogy and for her helpful insights in conversation about them. I owe to her the suggestion that Lisbeth's self-empowerment is partially related to her financial situation.

SECRET MEETINGS: THE TRUTH IS IN THE GOSSIP

Karen C. Adkins

The word *gossip* has a negative connotation and is conventionally defined as spreading malicious (often false) information about someone who is absent. Indeed, labeling information "gossip" or a person a "gossip" is a quick and efficient way to undercut authority from the outset. The standard ethical analysis of gossip, that of Sissela Bok, is devastating in its brevity—gossip's possibility is limited to "trivializing" and "reprehensible."[1]

Although illustrating gossip's negative consequences, Stieg Larsson's trilogy nonetheless defends the positive uses of gossip. Knowledge (especially through gossip) is power, for Larsson—both for good and for ill. In the novels, gossip is used as a tool of reputation (mis)management by those in power, as a way of maintaining power, and as a crucial means of getting information or drawing conclusions about a person based on limited information.

Larsson clearly defends gossip as a legitimate (even necessary) path to knowledge. Along similar lines, some contemporary philosophers have sought to restore credibility to gossip, defending the possibility of loose talk producing real knowledge. Maryann Ayim and Lorraine Code, for example, defend gossip as knowledge producing in part *because* of its looseness.[2] When we talk loosely, we can speculate freely, as do Blomkvist and Salander, creatively putting together different ideas.

Can I Trust You with This?

Gossip rests on a bedrock of trust—we must be able to trust someone with information, confidences, or secrets, to confide in them. (If we don't directly ask for confidentiality, we at least expect anonymity when we tell secrets.) Most professional people in *The Millennium Trilogy* are journalists and police officers who function by trading information, and they can be successful only if their sources are trustworthy. Larsson emphasizes the need for trust in those professions far more than we see in other crime novels.

The trilogy's beginning—Blomkvist's conviction on libel charges—highlights the importance of reputation and professional reliability. Blomkvist cannot function as a journalist if his public doubts his claims, or if he is simply repeating rumors, as the libel charge implies he's done.[3] Furthermore, his personal financial honesty is rightly identified by Salander as crucial to his professional success; he cannot be a financial scold if he's also revealed to be a hypocrite.[4] In the American legal context, reputation is valuable in part because it is seen as property.[5] Reputations can be destroyed or repaired through legal judgments, but they can also be destroyed or repaired through gossip.

In his villains, Larsson shows this concern for reputation. Part of why Gunnar Björck lines Bjurman up as Salander's guardian is because of his reputation and his disinclination toward gossip.[6] The absence of social capital or gossip can also be a marker of dissonance. Part of what turns the police inspectors' attention to Evert Gullberg as a possible Säpo agent is his complete absence of a professional reputation over an ostensibly long business career. In *The Girl Who Played with Fire*, what alerts the Section members that their surveillance of *Millennium* is outed is the complete absence of panicky staff talk about what to do with the supposedly empty magazine issue. During the many scenes of journalists discussing topics with sources, deals are constantly arranged concerning what is on or off the record.[7] And by the end of the trilogy, positions seem thoroughly knotted. In a reversal of the usual course of events, the police are an unofficial source for the crusading journalists *against* their own government agencies.

Obviously, high levels of trust are required for gossip networks to function. This makes sense, considering the word's linguistic origins—"god sibbe," a god sibling, an intimate friend of the family. Thus, in its original sense, "gossip" connotes intimate knowledge. Not surprisingly, then, recent scholarship makes a compelling case that gossip's evolutionary role is to confirm and enforce relationships of intimacy.[8] We can see the ways in which gossip is noticed, by its presence or absence, as a marker of intimacy. For example, Salander's friend Cilla Norén charmingly handles a hostile police interrogation about the Evil Fingers by pointing out that their "Satanic" get-togethers involve only beer drinking and gossiping.[9] Consider, too, that when Harriet Vanger withdraws after the sexual abuse by her father and brother has begun, her retreat is marked by the fact that she stops gossiping and confiding in friends.[10] If you can't gossip, you don't have friendships.

What's Mine Is Mine (Unless You Take It)

Gossip is often explosive because it makes private acts (more) public—we share information, ideas, or observations about people that aren't widely known. Much of the recent philosophical writing about gossip relates to ethical dilemmas concerning whether to reveal secrets, and, fittingly, the ethics of deciding whether to spread gossip is prominent throughout the Larsson books. Salander repeatedly makes decisions about whether to include information about clients in her reports to Armansky. Because she is a hacker, she has access to information most people assume is private, but she includes information only if she thinks it's relevant to the issue behind the report. Lisbeth says, "Everyone has secrets," and she is selective about when she reveals them.[11] Armansky has similar views on collecting information. He refuses to take cases from his business clients if the information they seek has nothing to do with their business. If a client's children are adults, Armansky thinks their personal lives are their own business.[12]

Ultimately, there are problems with this view of gossip and secrecy. Indeed, Blomkvist helpfully highlights the problems in his initial conflict with Salander, in which he contrasts his responsible use of private information with Salander's vigilante principles. "A bastard is always a bastard," she says.[13] Any damaging information, no matter how private, is useful if it limits the power of the bastard. Blomkvist's view of private information is one most people agree with (even while they endlessly read *People* magazine or check TMZ.com for licentious celebrity tidbits). Yet one moral defense of gossip lines up squarely with Salander's approach. According to John Portmann, "moral *schadenfreude*," pleasure in the suffering of others, is "(often but not always) an appropriate pleasure in fair punishment."[14] In line with this, Salander doesn't reveal private information endlessly or for the pleasure in its revelation. Her goal is to denature someone who abuses power in some way. She metes out what she sees as fair punishment.

Still, Salander's approach to secrecy is problematic, turning people into cases to be unfolded, objects to be examined, or currency to be traded (or, as Immanuel Kant [1724–1804] would say, more bluntly, mere means). Lisbeth is startled when Blomkvist first confronts her at her apartment. The person she'd seen as a "complicated computer game" was now in her home, her private space, and challenging her practices.[15] Larsson also suggests some hypocrisy in Salander's views; she is intensely interested in her own privacy, such that she regards personal discussions as "snooping around in areas she considered private."[16]

Scrutinizing others' private lives carries real risks and costs, and our own conviction of righteousness sometimes makes us thoughtless about those risks. *The Girl with the Dragon Tattoo* makes passing mention of the way in which one murder victim's relatives had his life destroyed when he was accused of murder.[17] And Portmann rightly argues that schadenfreude is morally indefensible when our motive is a sheer enjoyment of suffering for suffering's sake, rather than a pursuit of justice. Lisbeth is likewise immoral when she damages reputations simply for revenge. Consider her initial attempt to buy an apartment in Stockholm. When she is met with condescension, Lisbeth spends hours digging for evidence of income tax evasion by the dismissive real estate agent and then anonymously reports him.[18] She is motivated not by the pursuit of justice but by a desire for revenge.

The Grapevine Goes Digital

Normally, we think of rumor and gossip in purely oral terms—we whisper about scandalous behavior to trusted friends and confidantes. Yet the Larsson novels show how gossip works in the information age, both for better and for worse. Along these lines, Daniel Solove describes electronic gossip as publishing a diary, instead of hiding it away.[19] We can thus think of Lisbeth's hacking as electronically digging up diaries and sharing them.

Often relying on her friends for crucial information, Lisbeth is adept at working the gossip channels to subvert official reputation control. Her hacking is often a version of electronic gossip, discovering and disseminating information about others without their knowledge. Although Lisbeth often spreads gossip to clear her name, more generally she spreads gossip to defend underdogs against the powerful.

The hacker world of the Larsson novels and the electronic rumor spreading as resistance is a new historical phenomenon only in its scale and technology. For centuries, gossip has been an important tool of disenfranchised communities. One of the advantages of gossip and rumor generation is that it is available to all, including those with no access to power structures or publicity channels. Historically, there are many examples of oppressed communities using gossip as a means of challenging those in power: colonial Indians used rumor spreading quite effectively to organize and foment resistance to colonial rule.[20] Pre-Revolutionary Parisians snapped up censored gossipy *chroniques scandaleuses* and *libelles*, with their tales of monarchic abuses of private power.[21] Disenfranchised American blacks spread persistent rumors that AIDS was actually a CIA conspiracy to control the black population (with clear echoes of Tuskegee).[22] These examples, from across continents and centuries, demonstrate the persistent availability and power of gossip and rumor as resistance to more entrenched, official narratives about power.

When political print gossip becomes mainstream, the tones, salacious focuses, and extravagant commentary are similar to more traditional examples of gossip.[23] The only relevant difference between hacker gossip and these previous examples is that absolutely no trust is required to spread rumors on the Internet—anyone can click on a website and add critical information or forward a link to his or her contact list. Oral gossip and rumor rely on some basic trust in the reliability of one's source; newspaper gossip carries with it the reputation of the journalist. By contrast, it's very easy to set up an anonymous website, and forwarding a gossipy link carries with it less ethical freight than does spreading a rumor.

As we learn, Hacker's Republic is a closed community. Identities are often explicitly misrepresented, but in terms of character and core values, this is a deeply homogeneous group. Larsson makes this explicit when he notes that the hackers never spread viruses—they have no interest in interrupting commerce but merely want access to information.[24] Plague (who has set rates for hacking service) even performs a "pro bono" hacking for Salander so that she can find out who's sexually harassing Erika Berger.[25]

One of the obvious dangers of the free-for-all approach to reputation management is that reputational bells are hard to un-ring. Daniel Solove gives a host of examples of people whose momentary Internet fame, which comes often from completely random public moments (such as a woman who refuses to clean up after her dog on a Tokyo subway, or a young boy's school tape in which he pretends to be in *Star Wars*) are widely distributed and haunt them for years afterwards.[26] Blomkvist is a relatively benign example of this phenomenon: he is uncomfortable after becoming famous for his Wennerström article because one of the inevitable results of this fame is his becoming an object of reckless rumors.[27] Much more perniciously, after false psychiatric evaluations get Salander committed to state guardianship for years, the state initially proposes that she undergo a psychiatric evaluation to prove her competence (something that is normally assumed until the contrary is indicated).

When it comes to controlling one's reputation, there's a twisty trajectory from oral culture to print culture to Internet culture. As Walter Ong wrote, one of the truly remarkable features of the transition from an oral culture to a written culture is the development of the private self, with interior thoughts often sharply distinct from those of the public self (as indicated by the development of the diary and the epistolary novel).[28] The private self, in short, isn't some constant feature of existence or human nature—it has developed in history.

Gossip, as traditionally practiced only by intimates, becomes another marker of private space. One danger of the possibility of Internet gossiping and rumor spreading is that the private self has currency if its secrets are shareable.[29]

Small Talk about Big People

Blomkvist's gentle hypocrisy rests on the comfortable self-image of the powerful; those with institutional credibility always assume they use power responsibly (or, at least, assume that their uses and abuses of power can't be checked or discovered). Ultimately, part of the fun of the story is that we see Blomkvist move closer to Salander's views on gossip and privacy by the end of the trilogy. In *The Girl Who Kicked the Hornet's Nest*, he and Erika Berger are openly dependent on it. Blomkvist even tells Salander that revealing the most painful parts of her private life is the only way for her to regain control over her life. The girl who has sharply guarded her own privacy, while being cavalier about others' right to privacy, gets hoisted by her own petard.

The trilogy skillfully depicts the ways in which the powerful rely on gossip, while at the same time they deny its use and legitimacy. After Lisbeth is accused of murder, spreading rumors (primarily about her sexuality) seems to be the chief way of establishing her guilt—she is an unreliable, counter-cultural deviant. Section members are explicit about using the press to make their legal case—to damage Salander's reputation so much that her guilt will be decisively rendered, and legal proceedings will be mere formalities.

This tactic, of course, has a long (if not distinguished) pedigree. Demonizing women through gossip began in the Middle Ages. In the *Malleus Maleficarum* (a medieval church document of demonology published in 1486), gossip was a prime marker of a woman's status as a witch.[30] In this context, the public portrayal of Lisbeth as a Satanic lesbian cult member seems like a modern, Internet-enhanced witch hunt. Larsson's critique of how power structures work, particularly those in the worlds of finance and journalism, highlights the ways in which those in power use rumors and gossip to keep outsiders out. For people with access and the ability to disseminate information, gossip becomes a way to spread the indefensible defensibly. The very anonymity of gossip provides cover for those in power. Just as people who persecuted witches in the Middle Ages and in colonial New England were in fact those at the top of the social system, those who spread rumors about Lisbeth's behavior and cult membership also have the most public clout. This phenomenon of "official gossip" is all too common.

"Trust capital" is necessary for professional viability.[31] For instance, Blomkvist's critique of financial journalist-toady William Borg is as much for his habit of disparaging women and making jokes as it is for his journalistic weakness.[32] And Hans-Erik Wennerström comes to Blomkvist's attention initially because an old friend is suspicious of his reputation.[33] Anonymous sources spread rumors as a way to attack *Millennium* magazine's credibility and financial viability.[34] Even individuals less entrenched in structures of power use gossip in this fashion. Niklas Hedström gets angry that Salander has discovered his blackmail attempt of the impotent pop star he's guarding, and the only way he can think of to avenge himself is by "adding his contributions to the gossip about her in the canteen."[35]

Why I Can Trust You with This

Gossip is always infused with power, and Larsson focuses on friendship as a (potentially) ideal space that can transcend power conflicts. In this way, he's squarely in line with feminist treatments of gossip that ground its legitimacy in intimacy— we gossip only with those whom we know well and trust. Blomkvist's relationship with Salander begins on an adversarial note, with each attaining illicit knowledge about the other and using it as leverage. Blomkvist gets Salander to talk to him by pointing out that "he knows her secrets."[36] In this same scene, she strikes back by asserting that she knows everything; "knowledge is power."[37]

Despite their initial conflict, Blomkvist and Salander repeatedly put themselves at personal risk for each other and for their friends. Blomkvist in particular has a strong code of ethics for his friends: endless loyalty until they betray him, then they're completely done. This is also why he doesn't gossip about his friends.[38] Not everyone is so trustworthy. Consider that Berger's discomfort with her relationship with Blomkvist is chiefly that it makes her an object of gossip among her friends.[39]

Tellingly, Larsson closes the trilogy on a note of parity between Blomkvist and Salander. Salander lets Blomkvist in from her doorstep, in part, because "he knew her secrets just as she knew all of his," and because she trusts him.[40] It's not hard to imagine that she would find trust harder if the secrets went only one way. To trust someone fully, to confide in someone fully, requires a reciprocal exchange of sharing secrets.

Psssst. Pass it on.[41]

NOTES

1. Sissela Bok, *Secrets: On the Ethics of Concealment and Revelation* (New York: Vintage, 1984), pp. 94–101.

2. Maryann Ayim, "Knowledge through the Grapevine: Gossip as Inquiry," and Lorraine Code, "Gossip, or in Praise of Chaos," in Robert F. Goodman and Aaron Ben-Ze'ev, eds., *Good Gossip* (Lawrence: University of Kansas, 1994), pp. 85–105; Adkins, "The Real Dirt: Gossip and Feminist Epistemology," in *Social Epistemology* 16 (2002): 215–232.

3. Larsson, *The Girl with the Dragon Tattoo*, trans. Reg Keeland (New York: Vintage, 2008), pp. 14–15.

4. Ibid., p. 53.

5. Daniel J. Solove, *The Future of Reputation: Gossip, Rumor and Privacy on the Internet* (New Haven, CT: Yale University Press, 2007), p. 34.

6. Stieg Larsson, *The Girl Who Played with Fire*, trans. Reg Keeland (New York: Vintage, 2010), p. 382.

7. Larsson, *The Girl with the Dragon Tattoo*, p. 28; *The Girl Who Kicked the Hornet's Nest*, trans. Reg Keeland (New York: Alfred A. Knopf, 2010), p. 66.

8. Robin Dunbar, *Grooming, Gossip, and the Evolution of Language* (Cambridge, MA: Harvard University Press, 1996), p. 115.

9. Larsson, *The Girl Who Played with Fire*, p. 441.

10. Larsson, *The Girl with the Dragon Tattoo*, p. 211.

11. Ibid., p. 50.

12. Ibid., p. 36.

13. Ibid., p 344.

14. John Portmann, *When Bad Things Happen to Other People* (New York: Routledge, 2000), p.8.

15. Larsson, *The Girl with the Dragon Tattoo*, p. 329.

16. Larsson, *The Girl Who Played with Fire*, p. 31.

17. Larsson, *The Girl with the Dragon Tattoo*, p. 359.

18. Larsson, *The Girl Who Played with Fire*, p. 77.

19. Solove, *The Future of Reputation*, p. 59.

20. Ranajit Guha, *Elementary Aspects of the Peasant Insurgency in Colonial India* (Oxford, UK: Oxford University Press, 1983), pp. 250–251.

21. Robert Darnton, *The Forbidden Best-Sellers of Pre-Revolutionary France* (New York: Norton, 1996), pp. 76, 80, 223–224.

22. Patricia Turner, *I Heard It through the Grapevine: Rumor in African-American Culture* (Berkeley: University of California Press, 1993), pp. 154–163.

23. Gail Collins, *Scorpion Tongues: Gossip, Celebrity, and American Politics* (New York: William Morrow, 1998).

24. Larsson, *The Girl Who Kicked the Hornet's Nest*, p. 242.

25. I'm sure it's embarrassing to admit this, but I found the Hacker Republic part of the Larsson trilogy almost thoroughly implausible; I have no trouble believing in highly capable hackers, but it was hard for me to imagine a self-regulating community of hackers who'd ever be interested in hacking as public service. Obviously, the recent development of the Wikileaks website, its endless explosive political revelations in the name of transparency, and even the subsequent rumors and counter-rumors about its founder Julian Assange's sexual (mis)conduct demonstrate the complete naïveté of my view.

26. Solove, *The Future of Reputation*, pp. 29–49.

27. Larsson, *The Girl Who Played with Fire*, p. 42.

28. Walter Ong, *Orality and Literacy: The Technologizing of the Word* (New York: Routledge, 1982), p. 131.

29. Solove, *The Future of Reputation*, p. 59.

30. Jane Kamensky, *Governing the Tongue: The Politics of Speech in Early New England* (Oxford, UK: Oxford University Press, 1997), p. 151.

31. Larsson, *The Girl with the Dragon Tattoo*, pp. 29, 53.

32. Ibid., p. 16.

33. Ibid., p. 28.

34. Ibid., p. 156.

35. Larsson, *The Girl Who Played with Fire*, p. 324.

36. Larsson, *The Girl with the Dragon Tattoo*, p. 329.

37. Ibid., p. 331.

38. Larsson, *The Girl Who Played with Fire*, p. 553.

39. Ibid., p. 133.

40. Larsson, *The Girl Who Kicked the Hornet's Nest*, p. 562.

41. Thanks to Eric Bronson for his extremely helpful comments in revising this chapter.

PART FIVE

75,000 VOLTS OF VENGEANCE CAN'T BE WRONG, CAN IT?

Opposition brings concord.
—Heraclitus

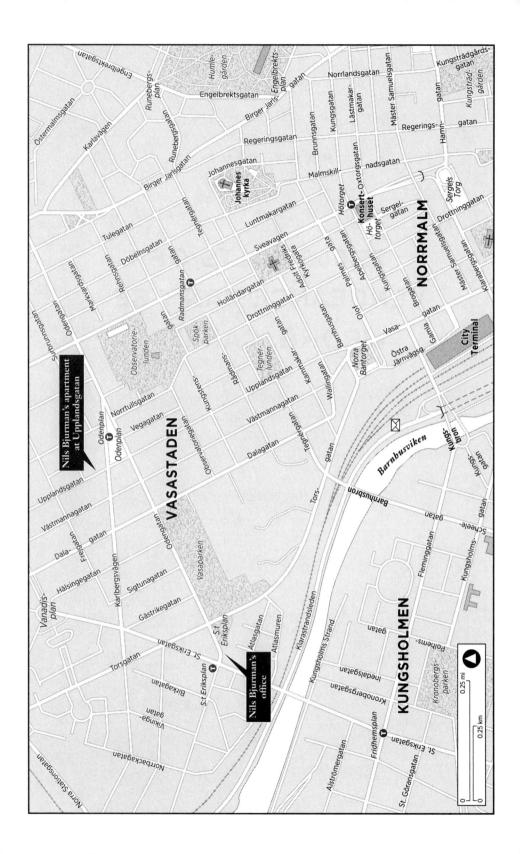

THE PRINCIPLED PLEASURE: LISBETH'S ARISTOTELIAN REVENGE

Emma L. E. Rees

Considering Lisbeth Salander's brutal revenge on Advokat Nils Bjurman in *The Girl with the Dragon Tattoo*, we might worry about our attachment to her. Why do we, as readers, continue to ally ourselves emotionally with someone who commits such an atrocity against another person? Do our moral compasses need resetting once we've entered Lisbeth's world?

Going back to fourth-century BCE Greece, we may better understand the fictional world of twenty-first-century Sweden. More specifically, taking Aristotle (384–322 BCE) as our guide, we can address our "heroine's" thorny ethical issues. Taken in isolation, Lisbeth's actions are, by the measure of a civilized society, vicious and immoral. Yet context is everything. Her systematic act of revenge on Bjurman, culminating in her tattooing I AM A SADISTIC PIG, A PERVERT AND A RAPIST on his abdomen, when understood as *consequent* to an original brutal act, is, in an Aristotelian sense, acceptable. Furthermore,

the pleasure we take as readers does not make us vicarious
collaborators or dormant psychopaths. Rather, our pleasure
marks us as Aristotelian connoisseurs of revenge. "It is equi-
table to pardon human weaknesses, and to look, not to the law
but to the legislator," Aristotle told us, "not to the letter of the
law but to the intention of the legislator; not to the action itself
but to the moral purpose; not to the part but to the whole."[1]
Context is everything when deciding what is "right" and what
is "wrong" in the novel.

Consider Bjurman, who has replaced the kindly but ill
Holger Palmgren as Lisbeth's guardian, and who therefore has
legal control over her affairs. Repeatedly in Larsson's world,
institutions that ought to protect their citizens are actually
complicit in their abuse.[2] Bjurman is, on the face of things,
a respectable representative of those institutions:

> Bjurman was apparently beyond reproach. There was
> nothing in his past that she could use. She knew beyond
> a doubt that he was a creep and a pig, but she could find
> nothing to prove it.
>
> It was time to consider another option.
>
> . . . The easiest thing would be for Bjurman simply
> to disappear from her life. A quick heart attack. End
> of problem. The catch was that not even disgusting
> fifty-five-year-old men had heart attacks at her beck
> and call.
>
> But that sort of thing could be arranged.[3]

In his *Nicomachean Ethics*, Aristotle offered a view that can
help us understand how Lisbeth's struggle for independence
in the face of her guardianship is defined: "a man is the origin
of his actions, and . . . the province of deliberation is to discover actions within one's own power to perform; and all our
actions aim at ends other than themselves. It follows that we
do not deliberate about ends, but about means."[4] Lisbeth's acts
of revenge against Bjurman are entirely consistent with her

desire to assert herself as independent in the face of the bogus manipulation of the guardianship order. Revenge is one "end," but a second "end" is achieving independence and producing a unified sense of self.

Punishment and Revenge

Lisbeth meticulously plans her visit to Bjurman. At this point—according to Aristotle, at least—she's planning *punishment* and not *revenge*. Might identifying an ethical difference between the two make us feel less guilty about applauding Lisbeth's actions—even to the point that we enjoy seeing them carried out?

For Aristotle, "passion and anger are the causes of acts of revenge. But there is a difference between revenge and punishment; the latter is inflicted in the interest of the sufferer, the former in the interest of him who inflicts it, that he may obtain satisfaction."[5] This idea of *satisfaction* is provocative: if the act of revenge is intended to satisfy the punisher's feelings, then aren't we punishers, too? By day, we might be thoroughly diligent and respectable professors, doctors, lawyers, business people, or students, but by night does our interest in *The Millennium Trilogy* mean we harbor fantasies of brutal retribution and harm? Do we collude with Lisbeth's brutal actions? Enjoy them, even? Is it okay to take pleasure from descriptions of ghastly activities if they're set up to be interpreted as being morally justifiable—even morally *necessary*?

Robin Hood, myth has it, did some ethically problematic (and illegal) things but was celebrated for stealing from the rich and giving to the poor. We applaud him because he is "sticking it to the Man." Lisbeth's story is similar. Her intention to harm Bjurman is nothing like the perverse self-satisfaction Bjurman took in raping her. Lisbeth's retributive act is far more complex. She is avenging herself *and* protecting other women (just as Larsson hoped he was by writing his books). As Aristotle told us, "he who commits . . . assault is guilty of wrong against a definite individual. . . . Being wronged is to suffer injustice at the hands of one who voluntarily inflicts it."[6] Bjurman has voluntarily wronged Lisbeth, and she can transform that injustice by taking her revenge.

Best Served Cold

Lisbeth goes through various options for disposing of Bjurman: a gun would be too easy to trace, a knife could be too messy and not efficient enough, a bomb, too complicated and not precise enough, and then there are numerous poisons to consider. She finally decides that she needs to gain control over Bjurman (to kill him could conceivably lead to a worse successor) in order to have control over her own life. So she decides to use herself as bait: "if she carried it off, she would have won. At least, so she thought."[7]

The plan goes wrong almost immediately. Bjurman quickly overpowers and rapes Lisbeth. Her intention had been to film him admitting to sexual assault and demanding sexual activity again (she could have used this recording for blackmail). As the situation develops, however, she ends up filming her own rape: "What she had gone through was very different from the first rape in his office; it was no longer a matter of coercion and degradation. This was systematic brutality."[8] Lisbeth comes to the realization that Bjurman has singled her out as his victim: "That told her something about the way she was viewed by other people."[9]

Lisbeth's second visit to Bjurman's apartment is altogether more successful. She stuns him with 75,000 volts from a Taser, and, once he regains consciousness, he realizes that the tables have been turned: he's tied spread-eagled to the bed. "Bjurman felt cold terror piercing his chest and lost his composure. He tugged at his handcuffs. *She had taken control. Impossible.*"[10] Because rape is a sadistic act, why is Lisbeth's violation of Bjurman's body not also categorically sadistic?

According to Aristotle, for an act to be *revenge* (rather than *punishment*), the individual being revenged-against needs to know who his or her attacker is: "men are milder if they think that those punished will never know that the punishment comes from *them* in requital for their own wrongs."[11] The guilty party should be conscious of the reasons for the revenge, which is why "we should inflict a preliminary verbal chastisement."[12] Lisbeth could have tattooed Bjurman when he was still unconscious, but that would have diminished the impact. Aristotelian revenge should satisfy the punisher's feelings and ours, too. As readers, we become vicarious punishers who are angry because we share Lisbeth's consciousness. This is not to say that we "hate" Bjurman, however. As Aristotle said, "Anger is curable by time, hatred not; the aim of anger is pain, of hatred evil; for the angry man wishes to see what happens; to one who hates it does not matter."[13]

Lisbeth's aim in inflicting this attack on Bjurman is, of course, revenge, but viewed through an Aristotelian lens it goes even deeper: the brutal act of revenge is the *only* rational, logical choice she can make for the sake of her future happiness. Such happiness is impossible in an Aristotelian sense while she's subject to the guardianship order, because independence is key to emotional security and well-being.

Rhetoric of Revenge

In both *The Nicomachean Ethics* and *The "Art" of Rhetoric*, Aristotle linked two phenomena that we might not think of as being connected: rhetoric and revenge. Aristotle was aware of how convincing rhetoric can move and persuade an audience. As readers of books or viewers of films, we are Larsson's audience. Larsson, then, is our rhetorician: we place our trust in him as he leads us through the convoluted plots of his stories. For us to *keep* reading or for us to stay in our cinema seats, we need to trust him, to believe that the emotional energy we expend on a character is not wasted and that our hopes for a character's well-being won't be betrayed.

In Aristotelian terms, if Larsson were inconsistent in his characterization—if he were to persuade us that a character deserves our empathy and then have that character do something utterly undeserving of our sympathy—then he would be an unjust rhetorician. We're swayed by our identification with the novel's sympathetic protagonists, by the structure of the plot, and by being in a receptive frame of mind for the persuasion to "work." If we were neo-Nazis reading one of the novels (an improbable scenario, I know, but bear with me), then we wouldn't be persuaded by Larsson's liberal rhetoric, and the narrative wouldn't *work* on us.

As judges, we can applaud Lisbeth's actions. In a court of law, Aristotle argued, "the speaker [Larsson] should show himself to be of a certain character and should know how to put the judge [us, his readers] into a certain frame of mind."[14] Furthermore, "when a man [in the twenty-first century, we can include "women" here, too] is favorably disposed towards one on whom he is passing judgement [Larsson/Lisbeth], he either thinks that the accused has committed no wrong at all or that his offence is trifling; but if he hates him, the reverse is the case."[15]

The ultimate goal for Lisbeth is to move from humiliation to a state of Aristotelian *eudaimonia* (happiness; a life worth living). "The very existence of the state depends on proportionate reciprocity," Aristotle told us, "for men demand that they shall be able to requite evil with evil—if they cannot, they feel they are in the position of slaves."[16] Revenge seen in these terms is a social and moral obligation: we will be condemned to servility if we *do not* take revenge.

We share Lisbeth's pain at the horrendous degradation she's suffered, and we celebrate the revenge that she has enacted, in effect, on our behalf. "We praise a man who feels anger on the right grounds and against the right persons," Aristotle argued, "and also in the right manner and at the right moment and for the right length of time."[17] In this interpretation, Lisbeth is not a crazed, violent misanthrope. Her violent revenge ensures pleasure both for her and for her fans. When someone retaliates, Aristotle argued, "there is an end of the matter: the pain of resentment is replaced by the *pleasure* of obtaining redress, and so his anger ceases."[18]

While Lisbeth and Larsson's readers experience this pleasure, it is an odd kind, because in achieving it, the pain of the initial injuries must be recalled. For Aristotle, pain and pleasure momentarily coexist:

> Let us then define anger as a longing, accompanied by pain for a real or apparent revenge for a real or apparent slight, affecting a man himself or one of his friends, when such a slight is undeserved . . . and lastly, anger is always accompanied by a certain pleasure, due to the hope of revenge to come. For it is pleasant to think that one will obtain what one aims at.[19]

Larsson depicts the revenge encounter as ritualistically cathartic for Lisbeth: "Then she went to the bathroom and washed. She felt a lot better when she came back in the bedroom."[20] It's *cleansing* for Larsson's readers, too, who identify with Lisbeth. For what Lisbeth has done to Bjurman to be in any way acceptable to us as readers (and by that, I mean that we're going to spend at least another 1,250 pages involved with her), we need to see things as Aristotle did, thus mitigating our collusive unease. Our rhetorician, Larsson, has inspired our confidence. In his persuasive storytelling, emotion has both dictated and shaped our ideas of justice. In his distinctions between anger and hatred, between revenge and punishment, Aristotle gave us the tools to argue that justice has been done. Lisbeth's actions are crucial for her self-preservation and, ultimately, for her happiness. Thus she is vindicated, and so are we.

NOTES

1. Aristotle, *The "Art" of Rhetoric*, trans. John Henry Freese (London: Heinemann, 1926 [Loeb Classical Library]), I.xiii.17.

2. See chapter 12 in this book, "Kicking the Hornets' Nest: The Hidden 'Section' in Every Institution," by Adriel M. Trott.

3. Stieg Larsson, *The Girl with the Dragon Tattoo*, trans. Reg Keeland (New York: Vintage, 2009), p. 240.

4. *Aristotle, The Nicomachean Ethics*, trans. H. Rackham (London: Heinemann, 1926 [Loeb Classical Library]), III.iii.15–16, p. 139.

5. Aristotle, *The "Art" of Rhetoric*, I.x.17–18, p. 113.

6. Ibid., I.xiii.3, 5.

7. Larsson, *The Girl with the Dragon Tattoo*, p. 244.

8. Ibid., p. 252.

9. Ibid., p. 253.

10. Ibid., p. 258.

11. Aristotle, *The "Art" of Rhetoric*, II.iii.16, p. 191.

12. Ibid., II.iii.15, p.191.

13. Ibid., II.iv.31, p. 201.

14. Ibid., II.i.3, p. 169.

15. Ibid., II.i.4, p. 171.

16. Aristotle, *The Nicomachean Ethics*, V.v.6, p. 281.

17. Ibid., IV.v.3, p. 231.

18. Ibid., IV.v.10, p. 233 (my emphasis).

19. Aristotle, *The "Art" of Rhetoric*, II.ii.1, p. 173.

20. Larsson, *The Girl with the Dragon Tattoo*, p. 263.

ACTING OUT OF DUTY
OR JUST ACTING OUT?:
SALANDER AND KANT

Tanja Barazon

Lisbeth Salander has peculiar moral standards. Her faithful friend Mikael Blomkvist believes she "has a delinquent child's take on morals and ethics."[1] It's surprising, then, that she shares some common ground with Immanuel Kant's (1724–1804) very traditional moral philosophy when it comes to bad guys.

In the first formulation of his categorical imperative, Kant wrote, "I ought never to act except in such a way *that I can also will that my maxim should become a universal law*."[2] To put it simply, I should never follow a rule of behavior that I couldn't rationally will everyone else to follow. According to Kant, the hypocrisy of the criminal still shows some level of rational thought. The criminal understands that laws must be enforced, and he certainly does not want to live in a world where he, too, must always fear attack. Yet the problem is that the criminal thinks so highly of his own rational skills that he firmly believes his actions should be considered exceptions. He wants to exercise his personal power but does not want his actions to be transformed into universal laws. Like Lisbeth, Kant detested the hypocrisy of the criminal.

Criminal Intent

The chief villains in *The Millennium Trilogy* are thoughtful people who hold high opinions of their own rational abilities. Take Martin Vanger. He might be the most morally deranged of all of the villains in the trilogy, but he is able to reason on a high level and possesses a wide range of practical skills. As CEO of a once-proud industrial powerhouse, Vanger must repeatedly lobby for support for his vision of internal change. "It's a patchwork quilt of alliances, factions, and intrigues," and it takes a subtle mind to keep it all together.[3] It's also why Vanger invites Blomkvist over for moose meat and vodka. Yet even in this initial exchange, Vanger displays an important clue to Blomkvist's investigation. As Blomkvist notes, Vanger "discussed the internal problems of his company so openly that it seemed reckless."[4]

When Blomkvist is invited down into Vanger's basement torture chamber, we get a closer look at Vanger's rationality. From his father, he learned to be careful and always cover his tracks. His murders, like his business decisions, are "not done on impulse—those kinds of kidnappers invariably get caught. It's a science with thousands of details that I have to weigh."[5] Vanger's talent for logical thinking is not at issue, but his hubris is. The Martin Vangers of the world see themselves as exceptions and therefore not subject to the laws of ordinary people. They believe they are entitled to "the godlike feeling of having absolute control over someone's life and death."[6] It is Vanger's bloated sense of his place in Swedish society that leads to his undoing. Because he "swung between rationality and pure lunacy," he cannot adhere to Kant's categorical imperative.[7]

Like Vanger, Hans-Erik Wennerström keeps a tremendous amount of information in his head. Every day he must make pivotal decisions to expand his empire, which "consisted of options, bonds, shares, partnerships, loan interest, income interest, deposits, bank accounts, payment transfers, and thousands of other elements."[8] While investigating Wennerström's transactions, Salander is forced to admit that much of his work has substance. Once again, we see a man who rises to the top because of his rationality and social skill. And once again it is reckless pride that does him in. Wennerström believes he is entitled to play by his own rules. Blomkvist is amazed that the "Mafia Banker" leaves a paper trail on his hard drive, but Salander and Kant know the criminal mind better. White-collar criminals, like petty thieves, do not believe their actions must be universalized. They believe they deserve special treatment. At critical times, people such as Wennerström "aren't very rational." Because Wennerström has so much pride in his rationality, he deludes himself into thinking "that the police would never think of confiscating his computer."[9]

Unlike Vanger or Wennerström, Lisbeth's guardian Nils Bjurman doesn't have an impressive command of rational thinking. When everybody's favorite spy-dad Zalachenko shows up at police headquarters, Bjurman is out of his league. As his colleague Björck observes, "To be honest, Bjurman was dead-weight. He wasn't particularly clever."[10] Still, negotiating the Swedish guardianship bureaucracy while moonlighting on occasional low-level Säpo jobs takes analytic ability, as does planning to have Lisbeth killed. Though the clumsy assassination plot only brings his own destruction, Bjurman "had begun to think rationally again" and knew "he would have to get his head in order," if he was ever going to get out of the predicament he had put himself into.[11] Ultimately, Bjurman's view of himself as an exception poisons an already dubious ethical code.

Heroes and Hacks

Lisbeth's actions are generally reactions to evil, but an important feature of Kant's ethical theory is that duty, not pleasure or self-interest, should be the motivation for action. There may not be anything inherently wrong about doing something purely for enjoyment, but for Kant, there was nothing necessarily ethical about it, either. Lisbeth repeatedly commits immoral acts for her own pleasure. She didn't start hacking into people's personal computers out of moral duty; she hacks because she likes it. "The truth was that she enjoyed digging into the lives of other people and exposing the secrets they were trying to hide. . . . It gave her a kick."[12]

Rather than go out and save the world, when given the choice, Lisbeth prefers to hide and be left in peace. Usually, she thinks of righting a wrong only after a perceived insult. When a real estate agent condescendingly tells her to come back when her piggy bank is fuller, she considers tossing a Molotov cocktail in his display window. Instead, though, she hacks into his computer and sends his undercover deals to the tax authorities "from an anonymous email account on a server in the USA."[13] Kant, on the other hand, preferred the more reasoned, emotionally distanced response to people, even when they acted like jerks. Officer Bublanski pays more careful attention to Kantian ethics:

> Bublanski was feeling an intense desire to reach out and grab the copy of *The Law of the Swedish Kingdom* that lay on the edge of Ekström's desk and ram it down the prosecutor's throat. He wondered what would happen if he acted on his impulse. There would certainly be headlines in the evening papers, and it would probably result in an assault charge. He pushed the thought away. The whole point of the socialized human being was to not give in to that sort of impulse, regardless of how belligerently an opponent might behave.[14]

Salander often falls short of this Kantian ideal, but she also works on becoming a better person. That's one important place where she differs from the bad guys she hunts. She trains her mind and her body to be prepared for everything. Kant said in his Doctrine of Virtue, "Cultivate your mind and body so that they are fit to realize any ends you might encounter."[15] Lisbeth not only works on her talents but also strives for perfection in every domain. Having refused to complete high school, she nevertheless develops her intellectual talents and abilities. As she tells Armansky, "I can handle anything and anyone you want, and if you don't have a better use for me than sorting post, then you're an idiot."[16]

Unlike the villains she chases, Salander sometimes puts her self-interest aside for a larger moral purpose. Blomkvist understands that "she's a person with a strong will. She has morals."[17] Salander agrees to do research for him because getting a murderer off the street is more important than the work she was doing for Armansky. Once she takes an interest in something, there is no stopping her relentless pursuit against injustice. It's why Salander is disgusted with Harriet Vanger. Vanger left Sweden to take care of herself and left Martin free to continue killing women for thirty-seven years. Salander thinks Harriet should have put her self-interest aside. It's also why Salander refuses Blomkvist's offer of half of the money he is to receive from Henrik Vanger. "I don't want one single krona from you," she tells Blomkvist, "unless it comes in the form of presents on my birthday."[18]

Practical Help

Kant's second formulation of the categorical imperative tells us to "Act in such a way that you always treat humanity, whether in your own person or in the person of any other, never simply as a means, but always at the same time as an end."[19] To consider the other person's humanity "not merely as a means but always at the same time as an end" means that you should not submit others to your advantage, using them or humiliating them, lying to them or stealing from them.

We must consider humanity as an end in itself in our actions toward other people. Of course, Lisbeth has to deal with many characters who don't do this at all. Zalachenko repeatedly treats people as means to an end. He uses Salander's mother for his own pleasure and abuses her when the pleasure wanes. He then uses his son, Ronald Niederman, to protect himself when Inspectors Modig and Erlander interview him in the hospital. Niederman is only a tool or an instrument for Zalachenko. Of course, Zala, too, is always being used for Säpo's benefit, thanks to his inside information about Russia. Evert Gullberg kills Zala for the benefit of the Section (and for the good of Sweden, by his own warped reasoning). Ultimately, by killing himself, Gullberg commits the Kantian sin of treating his own life as a means to an end, rather than respecting his own deteriorating body and humanity.

Salander appears to have trouble respecting humanity in others. Armansky is repeatedly put off by her long, unexplained, and unexpected absences from work.

> "I'll tell you why: because you don't give a shit about other people," Armansky said matter-of-factly.
>
> Salander bit her lower lip. "Usually it's other people who don't give a shit about me."
>
> "Bullshit," Armansky said. "You've got an attitude problem and you treat people like dirt when they're trying to be your friends. It's that simple."[20]

But Armansky is wrong, of course. It isn't that simple. Salander does care for good people such as Armansky and Blomkvist, even though she is terrible at showing it. She also cares for humanity in general, although the treatment she received makes her reluctant to open up to others. Still, Blomkvist knows that a promise from Salander is a sacred trust. He assures Harriet Vanger that Salander "gave her word that she would keep her mouth shut. I believe she'll keep that promise for the rest of her life. Everything I know about her tells me that she is extremely principled."[21]

The Injustice System

In Kant's system, the state should provide justice and therefore punishment for crimes. Yet what if we know perfectly well that the system fails us? The desire for justice is very strong in Lisbeth. "Unlike most other people who knew her, Palmgren was sure that Salander was a genuinely moral person. The problem was that her notion of morality did not always coincide with that of the justice system."[22]

Humans are interdependent. As Kant saw it, everyone should help everyone else because, obviously, we might need others to help us sometimes. Yet we know very well that this logic does not always hold up. Lisbeth believes that no one will help her. When Blomkvist proves that he is in fact very dedicated to helping her—supposedly because she saved his life in the first book—she never counts on it and is reluctant to be grateful.

Free will and free choice are two essential elements of Kant's moral theory. If an individual is forced to do something, then those actions cannot be called moral or immoral. Kant opposed welfare systems because they limit personal autonomy and treat people as if they were children, unable to care for themselves. When people need to rely on an outside power for their health or finances, they are not autonomous. As Kant was, Lisbeth is a champion of autonomy.

Lisbeth, however, goes beyond autonomy. Flaws in the justice system lead Lisbeth to take justice into her own hands in ways that Kant would not have condoned. She tattoos Bjurman because she knows that the police will not listen to her (although she considers that option and rejects it). The same goes for Wennerström. She not only steals millions from him, but is also secretly responsible for his murder. Taking personal revenge is certainly not Kantian, but Salander sees it as the only way to restore justice to a terribly unjust situation. Lisbeth does not concern herself with laws. Instead, she acts on a different moral imperative. In Kant's famous essay "On a Supposed Right to Lie for Philanthropic Reasons," he stated that we must even tell the truth to a murderer. Acting out of duty means not lying and not stealing, not even to protect a loved one, not even to save our own lives. In response to Kant's strict rule, Benjamin Constant (1767–1830), a liberal French philosopher, stated that we have the obligation to tell the truth only to someone worthy of the truth. This sounds more like Salander's moral code, which includes the principle that "a bastard is always a bastard, and if I can hurt a bastard by digging up shit about him, then he deserves it."[23] Lisbeth may not inspire us in the pursuit of moral perfection, but there is something deeply human and endearing about her. She does not offer herself as a paragon of morality. Like the rest of us, Salander is a work in progress.

NOTES

1. Stieg Larsson, *The Girl with the Dragon Tattoo*, trans. Reg Keeland (New York: Vintage, 2009), p. 384.

2. Immanuel Kant, *Groundwork of the Metaphysic of Morals*, trans. H. J. Patton (New York: Harper & Row, 1956), p. 70.

3. Larsson, *The Girl with the Dragon Tattoo*, p. 170.

4. Ibid., p. 186.

5. Ibid., p. 449.

6. Ibid., p. 448.

7. Ibid., p. 440.

8. Ibid., p. 555.

9. Ibid., p. 527.

10. Stieg Larsson, *The Girl Who Played with Fire*, trans. Reg Keeland (New York: Vintage, 2010), p. 528.

11. Ibid., p. 40.

12. Larsson, *The Girl with the Dragon Tattoo*, p. 332.

13. Larsson, *The Girl Who Played with Fire*, p. 77.

14. Stieg Larsson, *The Girl Who Kicked the Hornet's Nest*, trans. Reg Keeland (New York: Alfred A. Knopf, 2010), pp. 202–203.

15. Immanuel Kant, *Metaphysics of Morals*, trans. Mary Gregor (Cambridge, UK: Cambridge University Press, 1996), p. 155.

16. Larsson, *The Girl with the Dragon Tattoo*, p. 40.

17. Larsson, *The Girl Who Played with Fire*, p. 269.

18. Larsson, *The Girl with the Dragon Tattoo*, p. 559.

19. Kant, *Groundwork of the Metaphysic of Morals*, p. 96.

20. Larsson, *The Girl Who Played with Fire*, p. 140.

21. Ibid., p. 335.

22. Ibid., p. 150.

23. Larsson, *The Girl with the Dragon Tattoo*, p. 344.

TO CATCH A THIEF: THE ETHICS OF DECEIVING BAD PEOPLE

James Edwin Mahon

In an interview about *The Millennium Trilogy* in October 2009, Eva Gabrielsson, Stieg Larsson's partner of thirty-two years, commented, "The books clearly state that individual people do matter and may not be abused, lied to, misled or deceived for money, power or anyone's prestige."[1] That may be one of the moral lessons of the novels, but it does not mean that lies and deception may not be practiced for *other* reasons. Indeed, it is possible to read the novels as saying that people *may* be lied to and deceived, for the right reasons.

Both Mikael Blomkvist and Lisbeth Salander battle against those with power and money who lie to and deceive others. Yet both Blomkvist and Salander repeatedly lie and deceive. Blomkvist lies in order to obtain information, withholds information from the authorities, and deceives those who spy on him and (illegally) monitor him. Salander routinely violates the privacy of others, hacking into their financial records and private communications. She engages in fraud, theft, and assault, and lies about it to the authorities, even when the criminals are being brought to justice. Her rationale is that *"There are no innocents."*[2]

Blomkvist is portrayed as a good person, and Salander is surely not supposed to be a bad person. Did Larsson believe it was justified for Salander and Blomkvist to lie to and deceive bad people who are perpetrating crimes, in order to catch them? In any case, are such actions justified? Or, if they are not justified, are they at least excusable?

British philosopher J. L. Austin (1911–1960) argued that when someone is accused of doing something wrong, bad, or inept, there are two ways in which he or she can defend this conduct.[3] The first is to accept full responsibility for the action but to deny that it was wrong, bad, or inept. To do this is to *justify* the action, to hold that it was, in fact, the *right* thing to do. On this account, the action was *permissible* or even *obligatory*. The second way to defend the conduct is to agree that the action was wrong, bad, or inept, but to accept only partial responsibility for the action, or even none at all. To do this is to *excuse* the action, to hold that one is *not* (fully, or partly) *to blame* for how one acted. Consider an example. If I shout at a child, then my action may be justified (the child was about to touch a hot stove) or excusable (I have been unable to sleep for days, and the child is making a racket).

The question, therefore, is whether the lies and deceptions of Blomkvist and Salander are justified or excusable—or neither.

The Journalist Who Fights Fire with Fire

In *The Girl Who Played with Fire*, Blomkvist wants to help Dag Svensson with his book, to be published by *Millennium*, on the sex trafficking trade in Sweden. Svensson is trying to track down Gunnar Björck, officially the assistant chief of the immigration division of the Security Police (the Säkerhetspolisen, or Säpo), who has had sex with a number of kidnapped underage girls. Svensson has been unable to reach Björck. All that he has is a P.O. box address for him. Blomkvist asks Svensson if he has tried "the old lottery trick."

> "Think of a name, write a letter saying that he's won a mobile telephone with a G.P.S. navigator, or whatever. Print it out so it looks official and post it to his address— in this case that P. O. box he has. He's already won the mobile, a brand-new Nokia. But more than that, he's one of twenty people who can go on to win 100,000 kronor. All he has to do is take part in a marketing study for various products. The session will take about an hour and be done by a professional interviewer."
> ". . . You're nuts. Is that legal?"
> "I can't imagine it's illegal to give away a mobile telephone."[4]

Given Björck's crimes, given that there is irrefutable evidence of Björck's having destroyed "the lives of young girls against whom [he has] committed crimes,"[5] and given that Svensson has "tried everything else,"[6] it seems that deceiving Björck is permitted, in order to catch him. Such deception, it seems, is justified.

At their meeting, Björck strikes a deal with Blomkvist: in return for not being named in Blomkvist's story in *Millennium* magazine, he will give Blomkvist the information he needs about Alexander Zalachenko, the Soviet defector, murderer, woman-beater, and all around nasty piece of work. Blomkvist's deal might be thought to be immoral. Surely, given Björck's crimes, he should not be exempt from exposure and criminal charges, simply because he provides Blomkvist with information. Blomkvist, however, has no intention of keeping his word: "He did not intend to bargain with Björck either; no matter what happened he was going to hang him out to dry.

But he realized he was unscrupulous enough to do a deal with Björck, then double-cross him. He felt no guilt. Björck was a policeman who had committed crimes."[7]

After making the promise to Björck that "I won't mention your name in *Millennium*," despite the fact that he knows that Björck has committed crimes and that he is bound to report him to the police, Blomkvist defends his action with some moral casuistry: "He had just promised to assist in covering up a crime, but it didn't trouble him for a moment. All he had promised was that he himself and *Millennium* magazine would not write about Björck. Svensson had already written the whole story about Björck in his book. And the book would be published."[8] Blomkvist can keep his promise, and it will not be wrong to do so, because Björck will be exposed and prosecuted anyway, in the book written by Svensson and published by *Millennium* (but not in the article by Blomkvist in *Millennium* magazine).

Most people will probably condone Blomkvist's behavior here. The stakes, it will be argued, are serious enough to permit deception. Furthermore, Blomkvist can keep to the letter of his bargain with Björck, without protecting a criminal and a rapist from the police. (As it happens, Björck is murdered by the "Section for Special Analysis" or S.A.A., his former organization, before he can confront Blomkvist about his moral distinction). Indeed, some people may not be concerned about Blomkvist's ability to keep his word to Björck. They may sympathize with Blomkvist's original sentiment: no one should feel guilty about double-crossing a man such as Björck. Blomkvist's double-cross, if it is a double-cross, is not merely excusable, they may say. Given Björck's crimes, the double-cross is justified. Some people may even go further. If such a double-cross is necessary to get information about Zalachenko, then such a double-cross may be obligatory.

Most people will also probably say that the "double game" that Blomkvist gets everyone in *Millennium* magazine to play in *The Girl with the Dragon Tattoo* is justified.[9] The journalists pretend that the magazine is going under, in order to deceive the editorial secretary (who is working in secret for corrupt industrialist Hans-Erik Wennerström) into believing that they are not writing an exposé of Wennerström. As Blomkvist says, "I'm playing with the same underhand methods as Wennerström uses."[10] People will certainly condone the deception of the illegally eavesdropping S.A.A. in *The Girl Who Kicked the Hornet's Nest*. Here Blomkvist communicates disinformation over his bugged cell phone, and the entire staff writes a dummy issue of *Millennium*, in order to make the Section believe that they are not writing an issue devoted to destroying the Section and defending Salander. Blomkvist's private thoughts about this deception—which falls short of lying, because he is not speaking directly to his eavesdroppers—are noteworthy: "If nothing else, Blomkvist had learned from the preceding night's study of the history of the Security Police that disinformation was the basis of all espionage activity. And he had just planted disinformation that in the long run might prove invaluable."[11] He is now practicing espionage. He is behaving like a spy. He is doing what the secret police do. This behavior, however, is precisely the sort of behavior that he is dedicated to exposing in his journalism. The difference between the two, of course, is that Blomkvist lies to, deceives, and misleads not innocent people, but extremely dangerous, power-obsessed people who are engaged in a murderous conspiracy against innocent people, and he does so in order to prevent further murders and to bring the perpetrators to justice. Because of this, most people will consider his deception to be eminently justified, if not obligatory.

Salander's Principles

Lisbeth Salander's job in Milton Security is to investigate people's backgrounds for private clients. She does this by illegally hacking into their computers and taking them over, which allows her to read every document and e-mail (she is "probably the best in Sweden").[12] It is ironic that a person who is so intensely protective of her own privacy, who holds that her personal life is her own business and no one else's, is so eager to invade the privacy of others:

> The truth was that she enjoyed digging into the lives of other people and exposing the secrets they were trying to hide. She had been doing it, in one form or another, for as long as she could remember. And she was still doing it today, not only when Armansky gave her an assignment, but sometimes for the sheer fun of it. It gave her a kick. It was like a complicated computer program, except that it dealt with real live people.[13]

Although Salander likes to justify her digging into people's private lives by pointing to her success in exposing bad guys, it is not always the case that her subjects have done something wrong or illegal. Blomkvist, the subject of one of her investigations, is a case in point. When he confronts her about "the ethics of snooping into other people's lives," she replies, "It's exactly what you do as a journalist," to which he replies in turn, "And that's why we journalists have an ethics committee that keeps track of the moral issues. When I write an article about some bastard in the banking industry, I leave out, for instance, his or her private life. I don't say that a forger is a lesbian or gets turned on by having sex with her dog or anything like that, even if it happens to be true. Bastards too have a right to their private lives . . . you encroached on my integrity."[14]

Blomkvist's distinction between reporting on someone's corrupt activity and reporting on his personal life would appear to have merit, at least in cases in which the person's private life does not involve criminal activity. In response to his speech, however, Salander outlines her own investigative ethics: "In that case, it might amuse you to know that I also have principles comparable to your ethics committee's. I call them

Salander's Principles. One of them is that a bastard is always a bastard, and if I can hurt a bastard by digging up shit about him, then he deserves it."[15]

At least one problem with what Salander says here is that she can't know that someone is guilty of anything before she investigates him. She also doesn't know to what use the information will be put. As Blomkvist says, about her investigation of him, "Tell me this, when you were doing your research on me for Herr Frode, did you have any idea what it was going to be used for?"[16]

Even if Salander fails to justify or excuse her invasion of the privacy of others by means of "unlawful data trespassing," or hacking (not to be confused with the kind of sabotage that consists of sending computer viruses), it may be that people will forgive many of her other trespasses, given what she has suffered at the hands of others.[17] She lies to Nils Erik Bjurman, her new guardian, telling him that she simply makes coffee and sorts the mail at her job, and she invents a boyfriend for herself, "'Magnus' . . . a nerdy computer programmer her own age who treated her like a gentleman should."[18] People will probably consider such lies to be excusable, given how the authorities have illegally confined her in the past. (At this stage, Bjurman has not sexually assaulted her, although his questions about her sex life may be taken as an indication of his true intentions and may be enough to justify her deceitful response.) Her subsequent lie about being a student writing a thesis on "the criminology of violence against women in the twentieth century," in order to get access to police files, may even be seen as justified, given the importance of gathering the information for their investigation.[19]

The most worrying application of her principles in the first novel, however, concerns the cover-up of the horrific murders of Martin Vanger, the serial killer of young women:

> "If Martin Vanger were alive at this moment, I would have hung him out to dry," she went on. "Whatever agreement Mikael made with you, I would have sent every detail

about him to the nearest evening paper. . . . Unfortunately, he's dead." She turned to Blomkvist. . . . "Nothing we do can repair the harm that Martin Vanger did to his victims. But an interesting situation has come up. You're in a position where you can continue to harm innocent women—especially that Harriet whom you so warmly defended in the car on the way up here. So my question to you is: which is worse—the fact that Martin Vanger raped her out in the cabin or that you're going to do it in print? You have a fine dilemma. Maybe the ethics committee of the Journalists Association can give you some guidance. . . . But I'm not a journalist," she said at last.[20]

Blomkvist looks on this suppression of the truth as a "macabre cover-up," and it haunts him afterward: "The cover-up in which he had participated in Hedestad was unforgivable from a professional point of view."[21]

It is possible to understand why Salander believes that a cover-up of such a monstrous crime is justified. She holds that "bastards" are to be "hurt." In the case of the "bastard" Martin Vanger, there is no way to hurt him, because he is dead. Publishing a story on his decades of torturing and murdering women will not help any of his victims. Meanwhile, publishing a story about him and his father, Gottfried, and his sister, Harriet, whom they both raped repeatedly (until she killed her father and ran away from her brother), will hurt one of his victims, namely, Harriet. Salander believes that innocent people—and especially, innocent women—should not be hurt. Instead, she instructs the Vanger Corporation to "identify as many as you can" of Martin Vanger's victims and to "see to it that their families receive suitable compensation" and "to donate two million kronor annually and in perpetuity to the National Organization for Women's Crisis Centres and Girls' Crisis Centres in Sweden."[22]

There are at least two problems with this particular application of Salander's principles. The first is that she fails to

see any value in publishing the truth about Martin Vanger's
murders. The second is that she values harming those who are
"bastards."

Salander's harming of others—in particular, male, women-
hating "bastards"—is the one matter about which her normally
supportive former guardian, Holger Palmgren, gets angry with
her: "The only time Palmgren had been really upset was when
she had been charged with assault and battery after that scum-
bag had groped her in Gamla Stan. *Do you understand what
you have done? You have harmed another human being, Lisbeth.*"[23]
Mario Vargas Llosa has called Blomkvist and Salander "two
vigilantes."[24] Salander does seem to be a vigilante on occasion, especially on behalf of women, against the men who hate
them.[25]

Many people may consider her harming of "bastards" to
be excusable, given how Salander and other women have been
treated by them. Even if people excuse such harming, however, it is not at all clear that people will excuse the cover-up
of Martin Vanger's murders. Although such a story about his
many horrific murders could not help any of the victims, it
might help warn other women, and it could make it more
difficult for other mass murderers to operate, by alerting the
police and the public. Such a possible benefit—saving women's
lives—surely outweighs the distress that the story will cause
Harriet. Here, it seems, Blomkvist's judgment that such suppression is "unforgivable" is correct. It is neither justified nor
excusable.

Salander's principles are also supposed to exonerate her
from blame for lying to the police about what happened to
Richard Forbes during the night of the storm in Grenada.
Forbes, who is a wife-beater, is planning to murder his wife
on the island. Instead, during a powerful storm, Lisbeth hits
him, just as he is about to bash his wife's head open, and leaves
him on the beach. He later dies. He is another "bastard" who
deserves to be "hurt," with the true story being kept from the

police. Many people will consider such a lie excusable, if not justified. And her lie to Zalachenko (and Niedermann), as they are about to murder her and dump her in a new grave, that "Every word you've said in the past hour has been broadcast over Internet radio," is, no doubt, justified, because they are both "bastards" who are trying to murder her.[26]

The final novel in the trilogy, however, presents lies that are more difficult to evaluate. While preparing for her trial, Lisbeth tells her lawyer, Giannini, that "If I'm going to survive, I have to fight dirty."[27] She is referring here to her illegal use of a computer while in the hospital and her illegal hacking into other people's computers, including that of the prosecutor. Salander says that "if you get difficult about the fact that I'm going to use unethical methods, then we'll lose the trial."[28] Most people will approve of Salander's illegal actions, given that there is a vast illegal conspiracy working against her, and given that she is in this situation in the first place only because of multiple violations of her rights by agents of the state. Salander's illegal actions would seem to be justifiable.

What may not be approved, however, are Lisbeth's final acts of lying—her lying under oath in court and in her subsequent replies to police questions. In commenting on her autobiography, Lisbeth says that "She was careful to express herself precisely. She left out all the details that could be used against her."[29] In particular, she does not include the detail about shooting one of her attackers, Magge Lundin, in the foot with a gun taken from the other gang member, Sonny Nieminen. Nor does she admit that she went to Gosseberga to kill her father. As she says, "She did not mean to make their job any easier by confessing to something that would lead to a prison sentence."[30] Lisbeth lies during her trial and lies to the police afterward: "Salander lied consistently on two points. In her description of what had happened in Stallarholmen, she stubbornly maintained that it was Nieminen who had accidentally shot 'Magge' Lundin in the foot at the instant that she nailed him with the Taser. . . . As far as Salander's journey to Gosseberga was concerned, she claimed that her only objective had been to convince her father to turn himself in to the police."[31]

Both of these lies are told to policemen and policewomen who have finally acted to protect her against criminals. Both of them are told to men and women who do not, it seems, hate women and who are not "bastards." Salander's only reason for continuing to lie about shooting Lundin and about not intending to kill her father is her own welfare. She wishes to avoid being convicted of a crime.

It seems unlikely that she would be convicted of a crime in either case. The shooting of Magge Lundin could be said to be an act of self-defense and hence justified. If she did harbor an intention to kill her (murderous) father, nevertheless, she did not kill him. When she did injure him, later, after having been shot and buried alive by him, she only wounded him, and it was an act of self-defense.

Even if people approve of Salander's principles, it doesn't necessarily follow that they will approve of these final lies to the police. Like stealing 2.4 billion kronor from Hans-Erik Wennerström before revealing his whereabouts to his murderous pursuers, these lies may be neither justifiable nor excusable. The best thing that can be said about them is that Salander still considers the police to be untrustworthy. This might seem to be a harsh judgment, given that they have finally arrested all of the "bastards." Yet if it is still too early for her to trust the authorities, if she still considers them untrustworthy, then these final lies may also be excusable.[32]

NOTES

1. Eva Gabrielsson, quoted in Barry Forshaw, *The Man Who Left Too Soon: The Biography of Stieg Larsson* (London: John Blake, 2010), p. 25.

2. Stieg Larsson, *The Girl Who Played with Fire*, trans. Reg Keeland (New York: Vintage, 2010), p. 403.

3. J. L. Austin, "A Plea for Excuses," *Proceedings of the Aristotelian Society*, New Series, Vol. LVII, 1956–57 (London: Harrison & Sons, Ltd., 1957), pp. 1–30.

4. Larsson, *The Girl Who Played with Fire*, p. 165.

5. Ibid., p. 353.

6. Ibid., p. 165.

7. Ibid., p. 354.

8. Ibid., p. 515.

9. Stieg Larsson, *The Girl with the Dragon Tattoo*, trans. Reg Keeland (New York: Vintage, 200), p. 530.

10. Ibid., p. 534.

11. For more on how one cannot lie to eavesdroppers, see my "The Definition of Lying and Deception," *Stanford Encyclopedia of Philosophy*, http://plato.stanford.edu/entries/lying-definition/. Also see Stieg Larsson, *The Girl Who Kicked the Hornet's Nest*, trans. Reg Keeland (New York: Alfred A. Knopf, 2010), p. 144.

12. Larsson, *The Girl with the Dragon Tattoo*, p. 395.

13. Ibid., p. 332.

14. Ibid., p. 344.

15. Ibid.

16. Ibid., p. 333.

17. Ibid., p. 394. Salander is keen to distinguish between the two: "The citizens of Hacker Republic did not generally spread computer viruses. On the contrary—they were hackers and consequently implacable adversaries of those idiots who created viruses whose sole purpose was to sabotage the Net and crash computers. The citizens were information junkies and wanted a functioning Internet that they could hack" (Larsson, *The Girl Who Kicked the Hornet's Nest*, p. 242).

18. Larsson, *The Girl with the Dragon Tattoo*, p. 200.

19. Ibid., p. 362.

20. Ibid., pp. 513–514.

21. Ibid., pp. 514, 534.

22. Ibid., p. 514.

23. Ibid., p. 163.

24. Mario Vargas Llosa, "Lisbeth Salander debe vivir," *El Pais*, September 6, 2009, retrieved January 15, 2011, http://www.elpais.com/articulo/opinion/Lisbeth/Salander/debe/vivir/elpepiopi/20090906elpepiopi_11/Tes.

25. Larsson's own title for his trilogy of novels was *Men Who Hate Women*. While his Swedish publishers (Norstedts Förlag) changed the title of the trilogy to *The Millennium Trilogy*, he insisted that the first novel in the series retain the title *Men Who Hate Women* (*Män som hatar kvinnor*). He never had a chance to approve of the retitling of the English translations, which, for commercial purposes, all have "girl" in the titles. About the horrific murders of women by the serial killer Martin Vanger in the first novel and Salander's rape by Bjurman, Larsson wrote, "In the first book I created a serial killer by merging three real cases. Everything that is described one can therefore find in real

police inquiries. The description of the rape of Lisbeth Salander is based on a case that happened in Östermalm three years ago" (Barry Forshaw, *The Man Who Left Too Soon: The Biography of Stieg Larsson* [London: John Blake, 2010], p. 61).

26. Larsson, *The Girl Who Played with Fire*, p. 607.

27. Larsson, *The Girl Who Kicked the Hornet's Nest*, p. 321.

28. Ibid., p. 322.

29. Ibid., p. 318.

30. Ibid., p. 319.

31. Ibid., p. 518.

32. I would like to thank my father, Joseph Mahon, for introducing me to the novels of Stieg Larsson and for our many conversations about them and Larsson. I would also like to thank him for his comments on an earlier draft of this essay. I would further like to thank my indefatigable friend Don Fallis for his comments on the earlier draft of this essay. I read some of *The Millennium Trilogy*—or rather, the *Men Who Hate Women* trilogy—while traveling to and from Cannes, which is, of course, the setting of *To Catch a Thief*. I would like to thank my friend and fellow Duke alumnus Dara Sharifi for his hospitality, yet again.

CONTRIBUTORS

The Knights of the Philosophic Table

Karen Adkins is an associate dean and an associate professor of philosophy at Regis College in Denver, Colorado. Her dissertation and recent publications focus on gossip's contributions to knowledge; her extensive fieldwork in gossip as a functioning graduate student was crucial for this work. She identifies with the world of Larsson mainly through gossip and coffee dependence.

Tanja Barazon holds a Ph.D. from Paris Sorbonne University (Paris IV) and has translated Hegel and Bloch. She has created a new philosophical method called "soglitude-threshold thinking" and currently lives in Boston. She is working on a philosophical children's story about bears and telescopes called "The Mystery of the Planet Alas-K." Tanja is known to kick people in the stomach when they point out that she has a photographic memory.

Eric Bronson is a visiting professor in the Humanities Department at York University in Toronto. He has edited *Baseball and Philosophy, Poker and Philosophy,* and *The Lord of the Rings and Philosophy* (with Gregory Bassham). *The Hobbit and Philosophy* is forthcoming. Hacker Republic member and fellow Torontonian SixOfOne recently hacked Eric's computer and found a cryptically labeled database filled with incriminating, grainy photographs showing serious men in plaid shirts, playing banjos.

Sven Ove Hansson is a professor in philosophy and the head of the Division of Philosophy at the Royal Institute of Technology in Stockholm, Sweden. He is the editor in chief of *Theoria* and president of the International Society for Philosophy and Technology. He has published approximately 250 articles in international journals on topics that include ethics, decision theory, logic, epistemology, and theory of science. He is also an active critic of pseudoscience and can tell us why Larsson did not believe in UFOs, psychics, pyramidology, astrology, or even (gasp!) Santa Claus.

Andrew Zimmerman Jones is the author of *String Theory for Dummies* and the About.com Physics Guide, and a member of the National Association of Science Writers, American Mensa, and Toastmasters International. His Internet home can be found at http://www.azjones.info/. When not busy with his day job in educational publishing, Andrew attempts to hack life with his wife and two sons, who he hopes will grow up to be smarter than Lisbeth and more loyal than Blomkvist (though he'd happily settle for the other way around).

Dennis Knepp teaches philosophy and religious studies at Big Bend Community College in Moses Lake, Washington. His work has appeared in *Twilight and Philosophy* and *Alice in Wonderland and Philosophy*. Chapters in *Avatar and Philosophy* and *The Hobbit and Philosophy* are forthcoming. One night his wife strapped him down and on his chest tattooed this message: I AM HAPPILY MARRIED WITH TWO WONDERFUL CHILDREN.

James Edwin Mahon is an associate professor of philosophy and head of the Department of Philosophy at Washington and

Lee University, where he also teaches in the law school. In 2011–2012, he will be a lecturer in the Program in Ethics, Politics, and Economics at Yale University and a visiting researcher at Yale Law School. His primary research interests are in moral philosophy and its history. The son of Marxist academics who still teach in Ireland, James admires Stieg Larsson's politics but has no interest in dying before becoming world famous.

Aryn Martin is an associate professor at York University (Toronto). She teaches in the areas of science studies, sex and gender, and interactionism in sociology. Her research into bio-medical knowledge production and its incorporation into lived experience has appeared in *Social Studies of Science, Social Problems*, and *Body & Society*. A committed Mac user, coffee drinker, and nutcase, she finds a natural ally in Lisbeth.

Ester Pollack is an associate professor at Stockholm University and the director of the Doctoral and Master's Program at the Department of Journalism, Media, and Communication Studies. Her field of research is political communication and journalism studies. She has specialized in media and crime and in socio-logical and historical studies of the Swedish media. She has been the head of the department (2002–2005), on the board for the Swedish Organization for Media Scholars (2004–2007), and a member of the Board of the Faculty of Humanities since 2006. Ester actively participates in the Swedish public debate about the media's role in society, writes columns in a daily, and is often used by the media as an expert source. Her most recent project is a book about Nordic political scandals and the media, coedited with a colleague. She lives in the district of Söder in Stockholm, the stomping grounds of Blomkvist and Salander. Ester lives in a century-old Jugend building, which is regarded as an IKEA-free zone.

Emma L. E. Rees is senior lecturer in English at the University of Chester, United Kingdom. She is the author of

Margaret Cavendish and is currently working on her second book, *Can't: Revealing the Vagina in Literature and the Arts* (Routledge, 2012). She has contributed essays to four recent books: *Rhetorics of Bodily Disease and Health in Medieval and Early Modern England, The Female Body in Medicine and Literature, Studying Literature*, and, with coauthor Richard E. Wilson, *Led Zeppelin and Philosophy*. Emma spends any spare time she has with her husband, daughter, three cats, and dog. She spends any spare cash she has on going to rock concerts, the theater, and the cinema; on buying books and stationery; and on running a tremendously impractical but beautiful car. She is tattooed (no dragons, however) and pierced, and—like Lisbeth—visibly rebels against traditional standards of female "beauty." Unlike Lisbeth, the only apples she knows grow on trees, and the only hacking she does is when she coughs.

Tyler Shores has an M.A. in English from the University of Oxford and also a B.A. from the University of California, Berkeley, where he created and for six semesters taught a course titled *The Simpsons* and Philosophy (inspired by William Irwin's book of the same name). His research interests include philosophy, literature, and the impact of digital technology on the experience of reading. Tyler has contributed to other volumes in this series, such as *Alice in Wonderland and Philosophy, 30 Rock and Philosophy*, and *Inception and Philosophy*. He has also previously worked at Google and on the Authors@Google lecture series. Tyler spends his summers tending sheep at Cochran Farm in Australia.

Mary Simms was called to the bar of Ontario, Canada, in 2002. Since her call, she has practiced in civil and administrative law. Mary has gained particular experience in mental health law, representing psychiatric survivors before the Ontario Consent and Capacity Board and the Ontario Review Board. A virulent ABBA defender, Mary's greatest legal success was getting Fernando acquitted of holding a rifle in his hand (on "the frightful night we crossed the Rio Grande").

Kim Surkan is a lecturer in women's and gender studies at MIT, with research interests in queer and transgender theory, cyberculture, new media, and feminist philosophy. Having survived many Scandinavian-style winters while earning a Ph.D. in English from the University of Minnesota with a minor in feminist studies, Kim is now partnered and lives with a son and a daughter in a house filled with entirely too much IKEA furniture.

Andrew Terjesen received his Ph.D. in philosophy from Duke University. He has taught at Rhodes College, Washington and Lee University, and Austin College. Andrew has published scholarly articles on business ethics, empathy, and the history of philosophy. He is also an avid consumer of pop culture, and his meditations on its philosophical aspects can be found in numerous volumes, including *Mad Men and Philosophy*, *Avatar and Philosophy*, *Inception and Philosophy*, and *True Blood and Philosophy*. Andrew hopes to retire on the profits from his new cologne replicating Blomkvist's sex appeal, which he calls "Uncomplicated."

Jenny Terjesen is a human resources manager living in Memphis, Tennessee. Her explorations of the philosophical aspects of popular culture can also be found in *Twilight and Philosophy* and *True Blood and Philosophy*. Jenny loves coffee and sandwiches almost as much as Mikael Blomkvist loves women. But not more.

Chad William Timm is an assistant professor of education at Grand View University in Des Moines, Iowa. He earned a Ph.D. in education from Iowa State University, and his research interests include using postmodern philosophy to interrogate how students negotiate power relations in K-12 public schools.

Chad dreams of the day when his classroom will be overflowing with brilliant, sophisticated, asocial students labeled at risk of failure, like Lisbeth.

Adriel M. Trott is an assistant professor of philosophy at the University of Texas, Pan American. She works on ancient Greek philosophy, feminism, and contemporary political philosophy and has recently begun to focus on border theory. She has published on Plato, Aristotle, Luce Irigaray, and Alain Badiou. Adriel shies away from tattoos but not from dragons or hornet's nests.

Jaime Chris Weida is an instructor in the English Department at the Borough of Manhattan Community College/CUNY. Currently finishing her Ph.D. dissertation on science and mythology in modern literature at the Graduate Center/CUNY, Jaime also has a master's degree in physics from the University of Massachusetts and a bachelor's degree in astrophysics from Boston University. Her fields of interest include British and American modernist literature, feminist theory, queer theory, gothic and horror fiction, popular culture, and generally nontraditional and/or canonical literature. She lives in Parkchester, the Bronx, with her partner. While Jaime has no tattoos (not even one of a dragon!), she does have multiple piercings and usually wears black.

INDEX

Code Words

ABC News, 135–136
Abrahamsson, Monica, 57
accountability, 21–23
Addison, Joseph, 67
Aeschylus, 121–122, 125, 126
Agamemnon, King (Aeschylus
    character), 121–122, 126
Agamemnon (Aeschylus), 121, 125
Alcoff, Linda Martin, 34
"All the Evil," 110, 132, 133, 134
Alm, Cecilia Ovesdotter, 132, 134
ambiguity, gender and, 41–43
androgyny, 34, 35–37
Antifascistisk Aktion (AFA)
    (Anti-Fascist Action), 98
anti-Semitism, 96–97, 101–102. *See also*
    right-wing extremism
Arendt, Hannah, 160
Aristophanes, 121
Aristotle
    The "*Art*" of Rhetoric, 185
    catharsis and, 122–124, 125, 126, 157
    Nicomachean Ethics, 182, 185
    Poetics, 122
    revenge and, 181–187
Armansky, Dragan, 1–2
    education and, 20
    gender identity and, 35

gossip and, 169
    hacking and, 146
    labeling and, 13
    morality and, 193, 194
Arnold, Matthew, 115
"Art" of Rhetoric, The
    (Aristotle), 185
Asperger's syndrome, 7,
    42, 120
Assange, Julian, 141–142, 143, 146,
    150–153
astrology, 99–101, 103
Asylums (Goffman), 8
"at-risk" students, 20, 26, 27–29.
    See also education
Austin, J. L., 199
authority. *See* police; power
Ayim, Maryann, 167

Barlow, John Perry, 152
Baumrim, Bernard, 53
Beauvoir, Simone de, 71
Beckman, Greger, 52
Bentham, Jeremy, 26–27
Berger, Erika
    crime journalism and, 85
    education and, 25
    gossip and, 172, 173